SCHOLASTIC

SUMMER EXPRESS

S0-AZR-131

NEW YORK • TORONTO • LONDON • AUCKLAND • SYDNEY
MEXICO CITY • NEW DELHI • HONG KONG • BUENOS AIRES

Authors: Jennifer Moore, M.Ed. & Leland Graham, Ph.D.
Cover design by Brian LaRossa
Cover photo © MediaBakery
Interior illustrations by Teresa Anderko and Mike Moran

"Whales in a Noisy Ocean" (page 53) adapted from *Science World*. New York: Sep 1, 2008. Vol. 65, Iss. 1; pg. B4 © Scholastic Inc.
"The Race for Space" (page 95) adapted from *Junior Scholastic*. New York: May 7, 2001. Vol. 103, Iss. 18; pg. 16 © Scholastic Inc.
"A Dog's Life" (page 108) adapted from *Scholastic News*. (Senior Edition). New York: Jan 17, 2003. Vol. 71, Iss. 14, pg. 6 © Scholastic Inc.

Table of Contents

Dear Parent:

Congratulations! You hold in your hands an exceptional educational tool that will give your middle schooler a head start into the coming school year.

Inside this book, you will find one hundred practice pages that will help your child review and learn math, reading, writing, grammar, vocabulary, and so much more! *Summer Express* is divided into ten weeks, with two practice pages for each day of the week, Monday to Friday. However, feel free to use the pages in any order that your middle schooler likes. Here are other features you will find inside:

• A weekly **incentive chart** and **certificate** to motivate and reward your middle schooler for his or her efforts.

• A sheet of **colorful stickers**. There are small stickers for completing the activities each day, as well as a large sticker to use as a weekly reward.

• Suggestions for fun, creative **learning activities** you can do with your middle schooler each week.

• A **recommended reading list** of age-appropriate books that can be read throughout the summer.

• A **certificate of completion** to celebrate your middle schooler's accomplishments.

We hope you and your middle schooler will have fun as you work together to complete *Summer Express!*

Enjoy!
The Editors

Terrific Tips for Using This Book

1 Pick a good time for your middle schooler to work on the activities. You may want your child to do them around mid-morning or early afternoon when he or she is not too tired.

2 Make sure your middle schooler has all the supplies necessary, such as pencils, erasers, a ruler, and markers. Set aside a special place for your child to work.

3 At the beginning of each week, discuss how many minutes a day your child would like to read. Write the goal at the top of the incentive chart for the week. (We recommend that a student entering sixth grade read 30 to 45 minutes a day.)

4 Reward your middle schooler's efforts with the small stickers at the end of each day. As an added bonus, let your child affix a trophy sticker to each week's certificate for completing the activities.

5 Encourage your middle schooler to complete the worksheet, but do not force the issue. While you want to ensure that your child succeeds, it is also important to maintain a positive and relaxed attitude toward school and learning.

6 After providing a few minutes to look over the pages to be worked on, ask your child for a plan of action: "Tell me about what you'll be doing on these pages." Hearing the explanation aloud can provide insight into your child's thinking processes, and whether he or she can complete the work independently. If your middle schooler needs support, discuss which family member your child might prefer to work with. Providing choices is an approach that can help boost confidence and encourage your child to take ownership of the work to be done.

7 When the workbook is finished, present your child with the Certificate of Completion on page 143. Feel free to frame or laminate the certificate and display it on the wall for everyone to see— and celebrate!

Skill-Building Activities for Any Time

The following activities are designed to complement the ten weeks of practice pages in this book. These activities do not take more than a few minutes to complete and are just a handful of ways in which you can enrich and enliven your child's learning. Use these activities to turn otherwise idle time into productive time—for example, when standing in line or waiting at the bus stop. You will be working with your middle schooler to practice key skills and having fun together at the same time.

An Eye for Patterns

A red-brick sidewalk, a beaded necklace, a Sunday newspaper—all show evidence of structure and organization. Help your child recognize various types of structure or organization by observing and talking about patterns you see all around. Your middle schooler will be applying this developing skill across all school subject areas. The ability to identify patterns is a skill shared by effective readers, writers, scientists, and mathematicians.

Finding Real-Life Connections

One of the reasons for schooling is to help children function in the real world, to empower them with the abilities they will truly need. Why not put those developing skills into action by enlisting your child's help with reading a map, following a recipe, checking grocery receipts, and so on? Your middle schooler can apply reading, writing, science, and math skills in important and practical ways, thereby connecting what he or she is learning with everyday tasks.

Journals as Learning Tools

Journal writing is often associated with reading comprehension, but keeping a journal can help your middle schooler develop skills in many other academic areas as well. A journal can simply be a spiral notebook, a composition notebook, or sheets of paper stapled together. Writing and/or drawing in the journal will complement the practice pages completed each week. The journal provides another tool for monitoring the progress of newly learned skills and assessing those that need improvement. Before moving on to another set of practice pages, take a few minutes to read and discuss that week's journal entries with your child.

Promote Reading at Home

◆ Practice what you preach! You and your middle schooler should both read for pleasure, whether you like reading science-fiction novels or do-it-yourself magazines. Reading should not always be work. **Sometimes we should read just for fun!** Having reading materials around the house encourages you to read in front of your child and demonstrates that reading is an activity you enjoy.

◆ Set aside a family reading time. By designating a reading time each week, your family is assured an opportunity to discuss what everyone is reading. For example, you might share a funny quote from an article, or your child might tell you his or her favorite part of a story. The key is to **make a family tradition of reading— and sharing what you've read.**

◆ **Make a family collection of reading materials** that is easily accessible to everyone. Designate a specific place for library books and post the return date. This idea will save arguments and library fines. Buying used books or swapping books and magazines with friends and neighbors is another inexpensive source of reading materials.

Skills Review and Practice

Educators have established learning standards for math and language arts. Listed below are some of the important skills covered in *Summer Express* that will help your middle schooler review and prepare for the coming school year so that he or she is ready to meet these learning standards.

Math

5th Grade Skills to Review

- solving word problems using money values and decimals
- solving word problems using multiplication skills
- identifying equivalent fractions
- adding with regrouping
- adding decimals (e.g., money values)
- subtracting with regrouping and multiple regrouping
- subtracting fractions
- multiplying with regrouping
- multiplying decimals
- dividing with remainders
- changing decimals to fractions
- plotting coordinates on a grid
- recognizing geometric terms and shapes
- recognizing equivalent decimals, fractions, and percents

Skills to Practice for 6th Grade

- understanding the four arithmetic operations: addition, subtraction, multiplication, division
- converting/computing different forms of numbers
- problem solving
- exploring line and rotational symmetry
- converting measurements
- applying geometric concepts (determining angle measurement, circumference of circles, area of plane figures, and volume of solid figures)
- working flexibly with fractions, decimals, and percents
- applying strategies for computing with fractions and decimals
- utilizing appropriate graphic representation of data (circle graphs, bar graphs, Venn diagrams, and pictographs)
- understanding and applying basic concepts of probability and statistics

Language Arts

5th Grade Skills to Review

- using proofreading symbols
- recognizing forms of poetry
- writing for a purpose
- identifying and correcting incomplete sentences and run-on sentences
- identifying parts of a paragraph
- identifying parts of speech
- using subject-verb agreement
- punctuating using commas and colons
- summarizing or paraphrasing information
- using phonetic, structural, and context analysis to identify unfamiliar words

Skills to Practice for 6th Grade

- identifying parts of speech
- improving capitalization and punctuation
- improving spelling, vocabulary, and usage
- determining correct sentence structure
- summarizing and paraphrasing paragraphs
- writing in various modes and genres
- identifying figurative language and precise language
- using reference sources, including electronic reference materials
- using table of contents, index
- demonstrating knowledge of appropriate critical thinking skills (main idea, inference, sequence; reading for details, information, and understanding)
- correcting subject-verb agreement
- diagramming sentences

Helping Your Middle Schooler Get Ready: Week 1

These are the skills your middle schooler will be working on this week.

Math
- addition with regrouping
- interpreting a graph
- geometric shapes
- writing decimals
- money word problems

Reading
- reading for information
- sequencing

Vocabulary
- synonyms and antonyms

Grammar
- identifying nouns

Here are some activities you and your middle schooler might enjoy.

Start a Story Begin with a sentence that your middle schooler might say. Each player adds the next sentence, keeping the story line going but adding twists, turns, and characters. The challenge is to keep the story coherent, interesting, and somewhat complicated for the next player.

Get Moving Summer is certainly the perfect time to get in shape. So get out of your house and start a fitness program with your child that could even last all year. Try at least 30 minutes of aerobic exercise per day or every other day. You may also want to find some exercises for strengthening your muscles. Include friends and family in your fitness program.

Your middle schooler might enjoy reading one of the following books:

The House on Mango Street
by Sandra Cisneros

Call It Courage
by Armstrong Sperry

Black Holes (A True Book™)
by Ker Than

One Hen: How One Small Loan Made a Big Difference
by Katie Smith Milway

_____ **'s Incentive Chart: Week 1**

Name

This week, I plan to read_____ minutes each day.

CHART YOUR PROGRESS HERE.

Week 1	Day 1	Day 2	Day 3	Day 4	Day 5
I read for...	minutes	minutes	minutes	minutes	minutes
Put a sticker to show you completed each day's work.					

Congratulations!

Wow! You did a great job this week!

Place sticker here.

Parent or Caregiver's Signature_____

7/13/15

Add It Up!

Using what you already know about addition with regrouping, solve the following problems. You may use such strategies as mental math, place value, and regrouping more than once, as needed.

1. 932
    + 168
    ‾‾‾‾‾
    1100

2. 848
    + 254
    ‾‾‾‾‾
    1102

3. 672
    + 288
    ‾‾‾‾
    960

4. 222
    + 688
    ‾‾‾‾
    910

5. 4,358
    + 257
    ‾‾‾‾‾
    4615

6. 99
    + 387
    ‾‾‾‾
    486

7. 6,782
    + 19,803
    ‾‾‾‾‾‾‾
    26585

8. 98,388
    + 65,973
    ‾‾‾‾‾‾‾
    164261

9. 529
    1,140
    + 3,349
    ‾‾‾‾‾‾
    5,018

10. 3,009
    1,225
    + 17,791
    ‾‾‾‾‾‾‾
    22025

11. 1,234
    5,678
    + 91,011
    ‾‾‾‾‾‾‾
    97923

12. 4,562
    30,829
    + 16,049
    ‾‾‾‾‾‾‾
    51440

Having Summer Fun

First, read all of the ten sentences below.
Then number the sentences in proper
sequential order.

_9_ Jonathan and Ricky caught their limit
of fish for the day.

_5_ The boys put bait on their hooks and
wished the fish would soon bite.

_2_ Jonathan and Ricky walked down a
long dirt road to the lake.

_7_ When Jonathan pulled in the trout,
however, the fish wiggled off the hook.

_1_ The boys took their fishing poles and
tackle box with them to fish.

_6_ Jonathan was so happy because he was the first one to get a bite.

_4_ Ricky raced back to their cabin for the bait.

_10_ After the boys cleaned the fish, they enjoyed a delicious dinner.

_3_ When the boys reached the lake, they discovered that they had forgotten
the bait bucket.

_8_ Ricky was luckier because he actually caught the first fish.

Add one more sentence. What happens after sentence 10?

They went to bed.

Scholastic Inc.   Summer Express: Between Grades 5 & 6

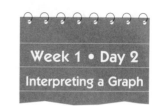

Weighing In

Use the graph to interpret the data and answer each question.

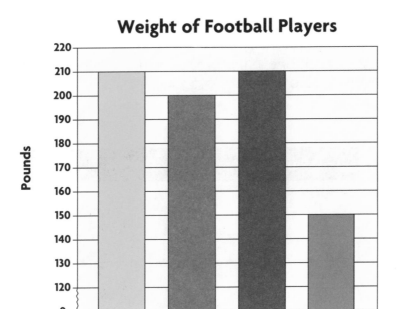

Weight of Football Players

Pounds

220
210
200
190
180
170
160
150
140
130
120
0

Jose   Mark   Cesar   David

Player

1. **What type of graph is this?** _Weighe graph_

2. **Which two players weigh the most?** _Jose, Cesar_

3. **How much does Mark weigh?** _200 Lbs_

4. **Which player weighs the least? How much does he weigh?** _David 150 Lbs_

5. **How many more pounds does Jose weigh than David?** _60 pounds_

6. **How many more pounds does Jose weigh than Mark?** _10 Lbs_

7. **What is the combined weight of Cesar and David?** _360 Lbs_

8. **What is the combined weight of all four players?** _770_

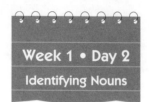
Who? Where? What?

A **noun** is a word that names a person, place, or thing.
A **person** may be a teacher, boy, girl, or lawyer, or someone's name.
A **place** may be an office, city, state, or aquarium.
A **thing** may be a nose, desk, ice, or love.

The words below are nouns. Write each one in the proper column to show whether the noun names a person, place, or thing. Choose the best category.

Noun

1. cabin
2. Kentucky
3. carpenter
4. year
5. lawyer
6. Abraham Lincoln
7. president
8. theater
9. speech
10. Indiana

Person	Place	Thing
Carpeter	Cabin	year
lawyer	Kentucky	Speech
abraham lincoln	theater	
president	Indiana	

Underline the **nouns** in each sentence.

1. Abraham Lincoln was born in a cabin in Kentucky.

2. He was elected to the Illinois General Assembly.

3. He became the 16th president of the United States.

4. While Lincoln was president, the Civil War was fought.

5. In November, 1863, Lincoln gave his famous speech, the Gettysburg Address.

Scholastic Inc. Summer Express: Between Grades 5 & 6

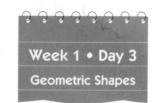
Get In Shape

Study the rules below. Classify each quadrilateral as a square, rectangle, rhombus, parallelogram, or trapezoid. Some quadrilaterals may have more than one classification.

Rules

Square	Rectangle	Rhombus	Parallelogram	Trapezoid
All sides are equal. All angles are 90°.	Opposite sides are equal. All angles are 90°.	All sides are equal. Opposite angles are equal.	Opposite sides are parallel.	One pair of sides is parallel.

1. _Square_

5. _____

2. _____

6. _Rectangle_

3. _Square_

7. _____

4. _Rectangle_

8. _____

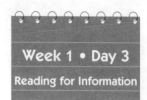
Read a Schedule

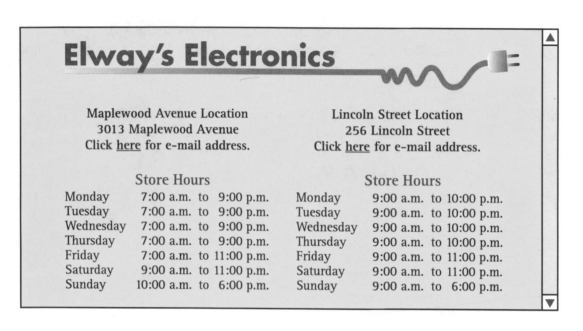

Elway's Electronics

Maplewood Avenue Location
3013 Maplewood Avenue
Click here for e-mail address.

Lincoln Street Location
256 Lincoln Street
Click here for e-mail address.

Store Hours		Store Hours	
Monday	7:00 a.m. to 9:00 p.m.	Monday	9:00 a.m. to 10:00 p.m.
Tuesday	7:00 a.m. to 9:00 p.m.	Tuesday	9:00 a.m. to 10:00 p.m.
Wednesday	7:00 a.m. to 9:00 p.m.	Wednesday	9:00 a.m. to 10:00 p.m.
Thursday	7:00 a.m. to 9:00 p.m.	Thursday	9:00 a.m. to 10:00 p.m.
Friday	7:00 a.m. to 11:00 p.m.	Friday	9:00 a.m. to 11:00 p.m.
Saturday	9:00 a.m. to 11:00 p.m.	Saturday	9:00 a.m. to 11:00 p.m.
Sunday	10:00 a.m. to 6:00 p.m.	Sunday	9:00 a.m. to 6:00 p.m.

Look at the schedule of store hours above. Then answer the following questions.

1. **How late can you shop at Elway's on a Saturday night?** _11:00 pm_

2. **Is either location open at 8:00 a.m.? If so, which one?** _yes, maplewood Avenue_

3. **Is either location open until midnight? If so, which one?** _no_

4. **Which location is opened the latest on Tuesdays?** _Lincoln street_

5. **Which location opens the earliest?** _maplewood avenue_

6. **Which location stays open the latest on more nights?** _Location street_

7. **Which location has longer hours on Sundays?** _Lincoln street_

8. **Suppose you want to know if an item is in stock before you go to the store. How could you contact the store to find out?**
   e-mail address

Scholastic Inc. Summer Express: Between Grades 5 & 6

The Same or Different?

Synonyms *are words that have the same or similar meanings.*

Antonyms *are words with opposite meanings.*

Examples: *difficult and arduous (synonyms); sincere and flippant (antonyms)*

Partner each word listed below in column A with the most appropriate and precise match from column B. Check a dictionary or a thesaurus if you are unsure of your choice.

Synonyms

Column A		Column B
d	1. express	a. lower
b	2. venture	b. travel
A	3. alight	c. earnings
h	4. routine	d. say
g	5. enormous	e. feeling
e	6. symptom	f. temporary
f	7. brief	g. grandiose
c	8. wage	h. regular

Antonyms

Column A		Column B
h	1. idle	a. anxious
a	2. nonchalant	b. calm
b	3. intense	c. exposed
g	4. narrow	d. spread
c	5. concealed	e. flexible
f	6. establish	f. close
d	7. gather	g. broad
e	8. rigid	h. active

After reading the following sentences, decide which word in parentheses is a **synonym** for the underlined word, and circle that word.

1. **The gymnast winced when the doctor <u>examined</u> her injured knee. (graded, observed)**

2. **The baseball game was an example of <u>superb</u> teamwork. (interesting, fantastic)**

3. **Our coach takes our team to professional games to <u>better</u> our game. (show, improve)**

4. **My dog is more likely to eat his food faster if he is <u>famished</u>. (hungry, sleepy)**

5. **I left a seat <u>vacant</u> for my friend who was arriving later. (open, broken)**

After reading the following sentences, decide which word in parentheses is an **antonym** for the underlined word and circle that word.

6. **I <u>often</u> bike while my dad runs a 5-mile route through our neighborhood. (daily, never)**

7. **My cousins live in an area where they can water ski <u>anytime</u>! (tempted, seldom)**

8. **I like to shop with my friends who are <u>extravagant</u>. (noisy, frugal)**

9. **I have to wear glasses in order to see things <u>faraway</u>. (nearby, clearly)**

10. **I hope to <u>sell</u> the rowboat this summer. (purchase, repair)**

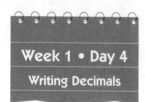

Every Number Has Its Place

Write each decimal in standard form on the lines below. Fit the number into the puzzle. The decimal points occupy one space and are already written in the puzzle.

1. **three and forty-four hundredths**

   3.4400

2. **four and six tenths**

3. **forty-one and seven tenths**

4. **four thousand sixteen and thirty-two hundredths**

5. **nine hundred forty-seven and thirty-six hundredths**

6. **six and five tenths**

7. **fifty-six and four tenths**

8. **one and thirty-five hundredths**

9. **one and six thousandths**

10. **forty-five and sixty-three hundredths**

11. **fifteen and three tenths**

12. **three hundred seventeen and nine tenths**

13. **three thousand seven and fifty-five hundredths**

14. **six and nineteen hundredths**

15. **six and ninety-nine hundredths**

Money Problems

Use the necessary operations, such as addition, subtraction, multiplication, and division, to solve the following money word problems. Do your work on a separate sheet of paper.

1. Kia and Luc had $20.00 each to spend at the mall. They planned to shop first, then see a movie. Kia bought a T-shirt for $12.38; her movie ticket was $6.75. Luc rented two video games for $1.50 each, and his movie ticket was $6.75. How much did each person spend in all at the mall?

Kia 19.13   Luc 9.75

2. Mark and Jon attend the same soccer camp. The camp costs $195.00 per person, per week. The boys also have to pay their own travel costs to and from camp. If the boys ride up and back together, they only spend $80.00 on gas. Find the total each boy will pay to cover camp and travel costs for a week.

235.00

3. Madison and Julia run a pet-sitting service for dogs. They charge $4.00 for dog walking, $12.00 for bathing, and $25.00 for overnight boarding. If a customer orders a bath with overnight boarding, the girls charge $30.00 for that combination. A new dog, Cash, is going to board overnight, have a bath, and go on two walks. What is the total cost for these services?

36.00

4. Frannie went to the local surf shop with $40.00. She bought some board wax and a skim board. The board cost $35.00, and wax cost $1.75. How much money does Frannie have left?

3.25

5. Mrs. Carney owns a restaurant. She has several lunch specials on the menu that are only $4.99 each. They include an entrée, a soup, and a beverage. This week, 72 customers ordered one of the specials. How much money did she make this week from the lunch specials?

359.28

6. Mrs. Kaye owns a small amusement park with a water slide, a miniature golf course, and a two-mile zip line. A day pass for the water slide costs $45.00. One round of golf costs $15.00, and a zip line ride costs $36.00. What will Mrs. Kaye earn today if she sells 5 zip-line tickets, 22 water-slide day passes, and 10 rounds of golf?

1,320

A Hopi History

Use the nonfiction passage below to answer the questions at the bottom of this page.
Refer to the passage for information if needed. Circle the correct answer.

The Hopi Indians are included among those Native American groups known as Pueblo Indians. Of the Native Americans living in the southwestern United States today, the Hopi have lived there the longest, residing in what is currently the state of Arizona. Their history includes remarkable inventions and arts that are still part of Hopi culture today.

Because the land where the Hopi live is dry and the climate is hot, irrigation has always been very important to Hopi farmers. After experience growing several crops, including beans and squash, corn was found to survive best, and they learned to use it in many different ways and in almost every dish they ate. However, the need to get water to their crops was still great. This need inspired the beginning of irrigation as we know it today. The Hopi created a system of water pipes to carry water from a distant river to thirsty crops. Thanks to the Hopi, modern day farmers give little thought to how they will manage to water their crops when there is little or no rain. This invention had an enormous impact on the work farming required.

The types of homes the Hopi built gave them shelter and also served as protection against attacks by an enemy. The houses were built in the recesses of the huge mesas and mountains because these openings were shielded from the elements and hidden from plain sight. The Hopi used the natural resource offered by the land: dry, dense clay. They made blocks from this clay and stacked them one on top of the other. When complete, a wall was formed—without an opening for a door! The only entrance was a tiny opening at the top of the wall, which they reached with a ladder that could be pulled inside the house in the event of danger.

The Hopi Indians had many rituals and customs to honor their gods. One such ceremony was the snake ceremony, which was performed by men in a special structure called a Kiva. The men collected snakes and then confined themselves—with the snakes!—in the Kiva for four days of prayer. After the fourth day, the men emerged holding the snakes in their mouths, then released the snakes into the open land believing the snakes would deliver their prayers to the gods.

1. **The Hopi Indians systematized farming through this process.**
   A. Pueblo
   B. ceremonies
   C. ladders
   D. irrigation

2. **Other than squash and beans, the Hopi grew crops of**
   A. pears.
   B. corn.
   C. clay.
   D. tomatoes.

3. **The Hopi built homes accessible only by**
   A. mesas.
   B. Kivas.
   C. ladders.
   D. pipes.

4. **The Hopi performed a ceremony honoring**
   A. snakes.
   B. gods.
   C. prayers.
   D. men.

Scholastic Inc.   Summer Express: Between Grades 5 & 6

Helping Your Middle Schooler Get Ready: Week 2

These are the skills your middle schooler will be working on this week.

Math
- simplifying fractions
- multiplication word problems
- mixed practice

Reading
- following directions
- sequencing

Writing
- job interview
- poetry: haiku

Vocabulary
- suffixes

Grammar
- parts of speech
- subject-verb agreement

Here are some activities you and your middle schooler might enjoy.

Map It Out Find a map and plan a real or imaginary trip with your child. Together, choose a destination and begin to highlight your route. Decide how many days it would take, where to stop, and what you would like to see or visit. Calculate the amount and cost of gas you would use based on today's gas prices.

Window Poem Encourage your child to write a window poem. Have him or her look out a window and write a short poem about what he or she sees. Your child can write directly on the glass by using dry-erase markers.

Your middle schooler might enjoy reading one of the following books:

In Memory of Gorfman T. Frog
by Gail Donovan

Little House on Rocky Ridge
by Roger Lea MacBride

*Polar Bear Math: Learning About Fractions
From Klondike and Snow*
by Ann Whitehead Nagda and Cindy Bickel

Listening for Lions
by Gloria Whelan

_____ 's Incentive Chart: Week 2
Name

This week, I plan to read_____ minutes each day.

CHART YOUR PROGRESS HERE.

Week 1  I read for...	Day 1 minutes	Day 2 minutes	Day 3 minutes	Day 4 minutes	Day 5 minutes
Put a sticker to show you completed each day's work.					

Congratulations!

Wow! You did a great job this week!

Place sticker here.

Parent or Caregiver's Signature_____

Building Vocabulary

 A **suffix** is a word part that is added to the **end** of a word and changes its part of speech and its meaning. For example, adding the suffix –er to read (a verb) makes the new word reader (a noun). Adding –less to face (a noun) makes faceless (an adjective).

Suffix	Meaning	Example	Meaning
-er	one who	bak**er**	one who bakes
	that which	dic**er**	device that chops or dices
-or	one who	debt**or**	one who owes a debt
-able/-ible	can be made/done, having the quality of	wash**able**	can be washed
		valu**able**	having value
		deduct**ible**	can be deducted
		sens**ible**	having sense

Write the word that is formed by adding the given suffix to each of the following words. Write a basic meaning of the new word. **Remember:** Check the spelling of the new word. Sometimes a letter is added and other times a letter might be omitted. If necessary, use a dictionary.

Example: win + -*er*   winner   one who wins

1. **like + -*able*** _____

2. **advise + -*or*** _____

3. **resist + -*ible*** _____

4. **bat + -*er*** _____

5. **depend + -*able*** _____

6. **write + -*er*** _____

Camp Counselor Job Interview

Ms. Starks, the camp leader, received your application for Junior Camp Counselor. She has called you in for an interview. The interview will be a chance for the camp leader to ask you questions. The questions might be about your family, friends, interests, possible future plans, as well as your job skills. To prepare for the interview, write out answers to the questions. Then ask one of your family members to interview you as if he or she is Ms. Starks. Your interviewer can also come up with additional questions. **Remember:** Answer using complete sentences.

✳ **What is your age and school grade?** _____

_____

✳ **How many people are in your family?** _____

_____

✳ **Where do you live? How long have you lived there?** _____

_____

✳ **What are some of your favorite hobbies?** _____

_____

✳ **What is your favorite sport?** _____

_____

✳ **What is your favorite game that is not an electronic game or video game?** _____

_____

✳ **Why do you think you are qualified for this job?** _____

_____

✳ **Have you ever had a job before? Tell me about that.** _____

_____

✳ **What are your plans for the future?** _____

_____

✳ **What would you like to be or do when you are an adult?** _____

_____

Scholastic Inc.   Summer Express: Between Grades 5 & 6

Geographic Wonders

What is the world's largest country? The largest desert? The smallest continent? Do this fraction match-up to discover the answers. Each geographic "wonder" listed below is followed by a fraction. Reduce the fraction to its lowest terms. Then correctly match it to one of the fractions in the right column and you'll find the name of the geographic wonder or its location. Write that name or place on the line.

Geographic Wonders			**Place**	
1. **World's largest desert**	$\frac{39}{312}$	_____	$\frac{1}{7}$	Australia
2. **Largest country (land)**	$\frac{2}{18}$	_____	$\frac{1}{5}$	China
3. **World's largest city**	$\frac{19}{38}$	_____	$\frac{1}{4}$	Canada
4. **Highest waterfall**	$\frac{100}{110}$	_____	$\frac{1}{8}$	Sahara
5. **Largest country (population)**	$\frac{6}{30}$	_____	$\frac{2}{3}$	Mammoth – Flint Ridge
6. **Smallest continent**	$\frac{3}{21}$	_____	$\frac{10}{11}$	Salto Angel in Venezuela
7. **Largest cave system**	$\frac{12}{18}$	_____	$\frac{1}{6}$	Nile
8. **World's highest mountain**	$\frac{3}{9}$	_____	$\frac{1}{3}$	Everest
9. **Second largest country**	$\frac{12}{48}$	_____	$\frac{1}{9}$	Russia
10. **World's longest river**	$\frac{5}{30}$	_____	$\frac{1}{2}$	Tokyo, Japan

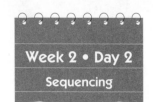

Jumbled Sentences

Rewrite the following words and phrases in the correct order to create a complete sentence.

1. wall   is on the   in the kitchen.   The clock

_____

2. for   the   city   bus.   Zachary   is   waiting

_____

3. Katie   piano.   is playing   the   grand

_____

4. living room.   in   the   There   are   mirrors   not any

_____

5. my   bed.   on   The   dog   is   sleeping   shaggy

_____

6. opening   the front door.   Aunt Margie   is   not

_____

7. are   Lei and Shane   looking   the right place.   in

_____

8. Jennifer   the   chapter of   is writing   novel.   last   her

_____

The Family Dinner

Do not read the story yet! Give it to a partner and ask him or her to tell you the part of speech under each blank below. You say a word for the part of speech, and your partner writes it in the blank. Then he or she writes the words where they belong in the story and reads the story aloud. Now you have created a hilarious story!

1. _____
   NOUN

2. _____
   (-ING) VERB

3. _____
   ADVERB

4. _____
   PLURAL NOUN

5. _____
   VERB

6. _____
   PAST-TENSE VERB

7. _____
   PLURAL NOUN

8. _____
   PLURAL NOUN

9. _____
   ADJECTIVE

10. _____
    ADVERB

Lei's family is Chinese-American. Once a week, they serve a traditional Chinese dinner. This week Lei invited her friend Carla, to have _____ with them.
                                    1

Lei's mother was very busy _____ dinner when
                                            2
Carla arrived. _____ Carla sensed all of the smells
                      3
coming from the kitchen. Lei's mother asked the girls to set the table.
The _____ gave each person a pair of chopsticks, a soup
            4
bowl, a soup spoon, and a rice bowl.

Carla asked, "Where are the knives and forks?"

Lei replied, "You won't need those. We always use chopsticks!
I'll show you how to _____ them."
                              5
Then the girls _____ into the kitchen where
                        6
Lei's father was chopping vegetables. Suddenly, he threw all the
_____ into a large cooking pan that was coated with very
        7
hot cooking oil. Lei remarked, "That's a wok!"

Lei's mother started pouring various _____ onto
                                            8
large platters. Lei asked Carla, "Will you help me take the platters
to the table?" Carla carried the bowl of rice to the table. There were
so many _____ dishes, such as stir-fried beef, steamed
              9
vegetables, sweet and sour chicken, and wontons.

Carla wanted to use the chopsticks but failed miserably. She tried
picking up a piece of beef, but it _____ flew across the
                                          10
table landing in Lei's father's plate. Everyone laughed but continued
eating the delicious food. Then Lei showed Carla how to use the
chopsticks.

Making Subjects and Verbs Agree

A verb must agree with its subject in number. Number refers to whether a word is **singular** *(naming one) or* **plural** *(naming more than one). A noun that is singular must have a singular form of the verb. A noun that is plural takes the plural form of a verb.*

Examples:

Cynthia enjoys cooking for her friends and relatives. (singular subject and singular verb)

Many cats sleep during the day. (plural subject and plural verb)

In each sentence, circle the subject. Then underline the verb in the parentheses that agrees with the subject.

1. The first TV system (was demonstrated, were demonstrated) at the New York World's Fair in 1939.

2. Early television sets (was, were) large black and white models.

3. Today, though, technical advancements (gives, give) us very high-quality color pictures.

4. Television (brings, bring) the world into our living rooms with pictures and sounds.

5. Almost all televisions (comes, come) with stereo or surround sound.

6. Until the 1960s, each city (was given, were given) only four or five TV channels.

7. Now, cable TV (brings, bring) hundreds of channels to our televisions.

8. A TV producer usually (decides, decide) which stories to cover in the newscast.

9. News photographers (carries, carry) video cameras to record, or film, the stories they cover.

10. A news item usually (lasts, last) between 20 and 90 seconds.

Scholastic Inc.   Summer Express: Between Grades 5 & 6

Banana Peanut Butter Treats

Using the recipe for Banana Peanut Butter Treats on this page, answer the questions below. This activity will test your ability to understand and follow directions. Circle the best answer for each question.

Banana Peanut Butter Treats

Ingredients
12 chocolate sandwich cookies
2 tablespoons colored sprinkles
4 firm, ripe bananas
¾ cup creamy peanut butter

Utensils
Large plastic bag
Rolling pin
Measuring cups and spoons
Pie plate
Spoon
Table knife
8 wooden pop sticks
Plastic wrap

Directions

1. Break the cookies into pieces and drop them into the large plastic bag.
   Securely seal or tie the bag. Use the rolling pin to finely crush the cookie pieces.

2. Put crushed cookies and colored sprinkles in the pie plate.
   Mix together with a spoon.

3. Use the table knife to cut each banana in half crosswise.
   Slide a pop stick into the cut end of each banana.

4. Next, use the table knife to spread peanut butter onto each banana.
   Then roll each banana in the cookie-sprinkle mixture.

5. Finally, wrap each coated banana in plastic wrap and freeze for 2 hours until firm.
   Makes 8 servings.

1. **Before the peanut butter is spread on each banana, what happens?**
   A. They are rolled in a cookie mixture.
   B. They are frozen for 2 hours.
   C. A pop stick is inserted.
   D. Each banana is cut lengthwise.

2. **How many different ingredients are used in this recipe?**
   A. 12
   B. 4
   C. 8
   D. ¾

3. **Which ingredient is used first in the recipe?**
   A. peanut butter
   B. bananas
   C. sprinkles
   D. cookies

4. **According to the directions, which utensil is used twice?**
   A. spoon
   B. table knife
   C. pie plate
   D. pop stick

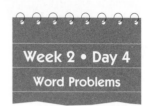
Multiply It!

Solve each multiplication word problem. Write the answer in the space provided.

1. **Each day after school, Carlos purchases yogurt and a banana for a total of $3.29. How much does Carlos spend on his snacks each week?**

2. **In July, the aquarium sold 5 times as many tickets as it did in June. The aquarium sold 987 tickets in June. How many tickets did the aquarium sell in July?**

3. **Peter saw in a newspaper ad that shirts were on sale at the mall for $23.45 each. If he purchased 6 shirts, how much would Peter spend?**

4. **Mr. Richards sold 140 bushels of apples. If he receives $15.50 per bushel, how much money did he earn?**

5. **Sally collected 7 times as many aluminum cans to recycle as Alan. Alan collected 2,999 aluminum cans. How many cans did Sally collect for the recycling drive?**

6. **Tony's printer is out of ink. Ink sets for his printer cost $18.49 for the color ink pack and $9.49 for the black ink pack. If Tony purchases 5 color packs and 9 black packs, how much will he spend in all?**

Scholastic Inc. Summer Express: Between Grades 5 & 6

Try Your Hand at Haiku

Haiku is a short, expressive poetry form that packs a lot of punch in just three lines! Haiku poems have a total of 17 syllables—usually 5 in the first line, 7 in the second, and 5 in the third. Traditionally, Haiku are nature poems and contain a season word. Have fun and try your hand at writing a couple of Haiku of your own! You can use the two poems on this page as guides.

Here are some tips to get you started:

❋ Choose a season (spring, summer, fall, winter)

❋ Think of a feeling or mood you associate with that season.

❋ List some seasonal words or phrases for your Haiku.

❋ Think of images or events you associate with that season.

❋ Write three lines totaling 17 syllables: 5 – 7 – 5

Example

Your Haiku

I love October!

_____

Red leaves swirl in autumn air

_____

A colorful dance

_____

        –LJ

Gold and glowing sun

_____

Sinks to cool in blue water

_____

Summer's long goodnight

_____

        –LJ

Practice Makes Perfect

Solve the problems below. Be sure to watch the operation signs. Use a separate sheet of paper to do your work if needed.

1. **776 + 459 =** _____

2. **640 x 30 =** _____

3. **8,200 – 5,389 =** _____

4. **6,043 x 8 =** _____

5. **63,105 – 4,345 =** _____

6. **21,845 + 13,000 =** _____

7. **33950 ÷ 7 =** _____

8. **508 x 739 =** _____

9. **89 + 43 =** _____

10. **4,666 – 1,888 =** _____

11. **551 x 530 =** _____

12. **4,001 – 1,999 =** _____

13. **8000 ÷ 20 =** _____

14. **347 x 403 =** _____

15. **21 + 24 + 52 =** _____

16. **8283 ÷ 251 =** _____

17. **9,000 – 4,578 =** _____

18. **7,288 – 1399 =** _____

19. **5535 ÷ 123 =** _____

20. **728 x 500 =** _____

Helping Your Middle Schooler Get Ready: Week 3

These are the skills your middle schooler will be working on this week.

Math
- addition with money
- subtracting fractions
- advanced computation

Reading
- reading for understanding

Writing
- narrative writing

Vocabulary
- prefixes

Grammar
- sentence fragments
- commas
- run-on sentences

Here are some activities you and your middle schooler might enjoy.

Book Hunt Have your child invite a friend or family member to the library or a bookstore to do a "book hunt." The two "hunters" will select five books he or she likes, and five that the other person will like. After 20 minutes, they should meet up to share selections. Are there similarities or differences in each of the hunter's reading preferences? Discuss.

Sports Page Make a deal with your child to follow a local or national sports team whose games, statistics, and players are reported several times a week. Read the sports pages each day and discuss your prediction(s) about what the team will do next. Explain why you believe that based on your readings. Perhaps other friends will join in next season.

Your middle schooler might enjoy reading one of the following books:

The Maze of Bones
(The 39 Clues, Book 1)
by Rick Riordan

Voices After Midnight
by Richard E. Peck

*The Escape of Oney Judge:
Martha Washington's Slave Finds Freedom*
by Emily Arnold McCully

_____ **'s Incentive Chart: Week 3**
Name

This week, I plan to read _____ minutes each day.

CHART YOUR PROGRESS HERE.

Week 1	Day 1	Day 2	Day 3	Day 4	Day 5
I read for...	minutes	minutes	minutes	minutes	minutes
Put a sticker to show you completed each day's work.					

Congratulations!

Wow! You did a great job this week!

Place sticker here.

Parent or Caregiver's Signature _____

Word Starters

A **prefix** is a word part that is added to the beginning of a word and changes its meaning. Learning prefixes is a great way to increase vocabulary; however, most prefixes are best learned in the context of the words that they create. Some of the most common prefixes are listed below.

Prefix	Meaning
de-	remove from, reduce
dis-	opposite of, not
in-	not
mis-	wrong
pre-	before
re-	again, back
un-	opposite of, not, to reverse

Underline the prefix in each word. Using the prefix chart above, write the meaning of the word in the blank. If you are uncertain of the meaning, look it up in a dictionary.

1. **defrost** _____

2. **preheat** _____

3. **disassemble** _____

4. **insensitive** _____

5. **deregulated** _____

6. **rewrite** _____

7. **preview** _____

8. **inactive** _____

9. **pregame** _____

10. **disadvantage** _____

11. **misunderstood** _____

12. **involuntary** _____

13. **incomplete** _____

14. **dethrone** _____

15. **reinvent** _____

16. **deactivate** _____

Garage Sale

The Moore family has the following items to sell at their garage sale on Saturday. Carefully study the list of items for sale before making your selections.

Assorted toy telephones (each)	$1.00	Toy tea set	$5.00
Animal puzzles (each)	$1.00	Fun sippy straws (each)	$ .25
Tennis racket	$3.00	Skateboard	$7.00
Assorted games (each)	$1.00	Paperback books (each)	$ .50
Lava lamp	$5.00	Bicycle	$8.00
Footballs (each)	$2.50	Pogo stick	$4.00
Football helmet	$3.00	Roller blades	$5.00
Doll carriage	$2.50	Baseball cards (sets of 3)	$1.50
Stuffed teddy bear	$2.00	Action figures (each)	$2.00
Various CDs, videos games (each)	$1.00	Dartboard set	$4.00

If you had $10.00 to spend at the garage sale, what would you buy? Keep track of the items you purchase and the total amount you spend.

Item/Number Purchased	Amount of Purchase
_____	_____
_____	_____
_____	_____
_____	_____
_____	_____
_____	_____
_____	_____
_____	_____

Total Amount Spent _____

Scholastic Inc.   Summer Express: Between Grades 5 & 6

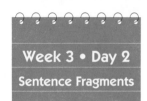
Complete Thoughts—or Not?

A **sentence** *must have both a subject and predicate (verb) to express a complete thought. A group of words that lacks a subject or a predicate (or sometimes both) is a* **sentence fragment***. A fragment does* **not** *express a complete thought and must be avoided in writing.*

Examples:

Found a wallet and took it to the lost and found department. (lacks a subject)

The ponies and horses in the barn. (lacks a predicate, or verb)

Into the goldfish pond. (lacks a subject and a predicate)

Draw one line under the complete subject and two lines under the complete predicate of each complete sentence. If a sentence is not complete, write **F** (fragment) in the blank. If the sentence has both a subject and predicate and expresses a complete thought, write **S** (sentence).

_____ 1. **I would like to take a kitten home.**

_____ 2. **Arrived at the county fair before him.**

_____ 3. **Isabelle's cat won the first-place prize.**

_____ 4. **Raises rabbits and birds in her backyard.**

_____ 5. **The biggest tomato and cantaloupe on the table.**

_____ 6. **Mr. Pickens received a blue ribbon for his prize cantaloupes.**

_____ 7. **At the county fair, won first prize for her quilt.**

_____ 8. **Martha made the squares for the quilt from her brother's old shirts.**

_____ 9. **At the dog show, my next door neighbor.**

_____ 10. **The ponies and the horses in the barn.**

_____ 11. **Richie won a stuffed gorilla at the county fair.**

_____ 12. **The cotton candy and popcorn were my favorites at the county fair.**

Conquering Commas

 Commas serve many purposes. *Use a comma (,)*

1. *to separate three or more items in a series.*
   Example: Ryan ordered a steak, baked potato, salad, and tea.

2. *to show a pause after an interjection or introductory word such as no, yes, or well.*
   Example: Yes, the sixth grade students will assemble first for the program.

3. *to separate the name of a person being directly addressed.*
   Example: Marcia, did you finish washing the dishes?

4. *before a conjunction (and, but, or) when the word is used to join two simple sentences with different subjects.*
   Example: My brother designed the tree house, and I built it.

5. *between a quotation and the rest of the sentence.*
   Example: "Your clothes are almost dry," said Mother.

6. *to set an appositive (word or phrase that renames the noun or pronoun in front of it) apart from the rest of the sentence.*
   Example: Mr. Parker, our neighbor, borrowed our lawn mower.

Read the sentences. Place commas where needed in each sentence and identify the purpose from the list above. Write that number on the line at the end of the sentence.

Purpose

1. **Clark you had better finish reading your book before Monday.** _____

2. **Yes poison ivy will make your skin itch.** _____

3. **Poison ivy looks like a shrub a vine or a small plant.** _____

4. **My favorite book *Charlie and the Chocolate Factory* has been made into a movie.** _____

5. **Grandmother said "I am so glad that you finished cleaning your room."** _____

6. **Cesar ordered soup salad bread and dessert at the restaurant.** _____

7. **My aunt drove us to the shoe store but we did not buy any shoes.** _____

8. **No I have not finished painting the garage.** _____

Scholastic Inc.   *Summer Express: Between Grades 5 & 6*

Fraction Subtraction

Find each difference. Reduce. Study the example below.

Example:

$$6\frac{2}{3} = \frac{20}{3} \times \frac{4}{4} = \frac{80}{12}$$

$$-3\frac{1}{4} = \frac{13}{4} \times \frac{3}{3} = \frac{39}{12}$$

$$\frac{41}{12} = 3\frac{5}{12}$$

1. Change any mixed numbers to improper fractions.
2. Find the least common denominator and rewrite fraction.
3. Subtract. Reduce if necessary.

1. $8\frac{3}{4}$
   $-4\frac{2}{3}$
   _____

4. $16\frac{5}{8}$
   $-4\frac{3}{4}$
   _____

7. $6\frac{1}{2}$
   $-5\frac{1}{3}$
   _____

2. $10\frac{1}{3}$
   $-2\frac{2}{5}$
   _____

5. $8\frac{1}{2}$
   $-3\frac{2}{7}$
   _____

8. $14\frac{3}{8}$
   $-5\frac{3}{4}$
   _____

3. $9\frac{4}{5}$
   $-7\frac{6}{10}$
   _____

6. $8\frac{9}{10}$
   $-3\frac{2}{5}$
   _____

9. $12\frac{1}{2}$
   $-3\frac{1}{4}$
   _____

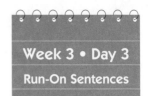
Fixing Run-On Sentences

A **run-on sentence** *is a sentence with at least two independent clauses (complete sentences or thoughts) that are forced together instead of being properly connected or separated.*

To correct run-on sentences, there are several options:
1. Separate clauses using punctuation.
2. Separate clauses using a conjunction.
3. Rearrange the sentence (by adding or removing words).

Example: Lauren smeared sunscreen on her arms and face, the sun was extremely hot.

Corrected form: Lauren smeared sunscreen on her arms and face because the sun was extremely hot.

Example: Walker received a new puppy for his birthday he named the puppy Rover.

Corrected form: Walker received a new puppy for his birthday. He named it Rover.

Correct the following run-on sentences by using any of the above options.

1. **Melinda likes reading mystery novels it sometimes makes her sleepy.**

   _____

2. **When I am older I want to have a big family, I really like big families.**

   _____

3. **Christine looked out the window she saw that it was raining.**

   _____

4. **Our family usually leaves for the park at 10:30 today we are going at 10:00 instead.**

   _____

5. **To make this project you will need 15 index cards you will also need several colored markers**

   _____

Scholastic Inc. · *Summer Express: Between Grades 5 & 6*

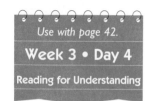
Fighting for Their Lives

Amazon Basin, Brazil – The Yanomami Indians in northern Brazil think it is the end of the world. And for the remaining 9,000 tribe members, it could be. Recently, fires raging in the rain forests endangered the Yanomami's homes, food supply, and health. But the fires are not the only threat to the Yanomami and other tribal people living in the Amazon rain forest.

Lumber companies are cutting down trees. Mining companies are digging up the land for gold. Gold was discovered on the Yanomami reserve in the 1980s. About 20,000 miners descended on the area. The miners brought diseases that killed many of the native people.

The Yanomami live in the secluded rain forests and scattered grasslands along the Brazil-Venezuela border. Their culture is very old; it dates back 3,000 years. The life of the tribe has not changed much in all that time. Some Yanomami had no direct contact with the outside world until last decade.

The Juma people also live in the Amazon rain forests. Less than 100 years ago, there were thousands of Juma living in the forests. Now only six Juma remain. The Juma still eat traditional foods and hunt with bows and arrows. Since they have contact with the outside world, it is common for them to wear modern clothing. Recently, the last young Juma warrior was killed by a jaguar.

"The Yanomami are heading for where the Juma are now," says Pam Kraft, who educates the public about native people. There are 250 million indigenous, or native, people who belong to endangered tribes around the world. The basic human rights of these people are recognized, but their rights to their land, their resources, and their culture are not.

Firefighters from all over the world flew to Brazil in response to the fire threatening the homes of the Yanomami. In the jungle, the tribal people held ceremonies, praying for rain to come and quench the fire. The rains came and began to extinguish the flames. The threat of the fire is over, but the Yanomami still face many urgent problems. They are still in danger.

"The future of these people is related to our behavior," says Sydney Posseulo, of the Federal Indian Bureau in Brazil. "We have to show more support for their way of life."

Circle the letter with the best answer for each question.

1. **Why have the Yanomami remained mostly unchanged for 3,000 years?**
   A. They've had no reason to leave their lands.
   B. They live without outside influences.
   C. They weren't allowed to leave the forests.
   D. They didn't know about modern tools and conveniences.

2. **How did the discovery of gold cause the deaths of many Yanomami?**
   A. They caught diseases from the miners.
   B. The miners killed the Yanomami to get the gold.
   C. The Yanomami moved off their land.
   D. The Yanomami died of starvation.

3. **What does "The Yanomami are heading for where the Juma are now" mean?**
   A. The Yanomami will live near the Juma.
   B. The Yanomami tribe will soon be as close to extinction as the Juma tribe is now.
   C. The Yanomami tribe is going the wrong way.
   D. The Yanomami and Juma travel together.

4. **How were the fires in the rain forests finally extinguished?**
   A. Firefighters flew to Brazil.
   B. Tribal people prayed.
   C. People held ceremonies.
   D. The rains came.

Circle the letter with the best definition of the underlined word.

5. **Many people don't recognize the tribes' rights to the resources of their land.**
   A. things available to use
   B. traditional clothing
   C. culture
   D. music

6. **Firefighters from all over the world flew to Brazil in response to the fire.**
   A. refusal
   B. fear
   C. quiet manner
   D. reaction or reply

7. **Mining companies arrived when they heard there was gold in the rain forest.**
   A. having to do with fires
   B. having to do with extinction
   C. having to do with digging for minerals or metals
   D. having to do with rain forests

8. **The rains came and began to extinguish the flames.**
   A. spread
   B. put out
   C. increase
   D. avoid

Create a Superhero

Create your own superhero! Describe your superhero's powers or strengths. However, give your superhero one weakness. Describe the weakness and how he or she would keep it a secret or overcome it. On a separate sheet of paper, sketch your superhero in action!

_____

_____

_____

_____

_____

_____

_____

_____

_____

_____

_____

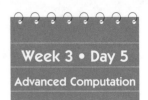

What's in a Name?

The tables below show every letter of the alphabet partnered with a numeric value. Use this "code" to determine how much your name would be worth by spelling your name and jotting down the value for each letter in it. Then add those numbers to get your total "name value." Try calculating the name values or your friends and family, too.

A	B	C	D	E	F	G	H	I	J	K	L	M
765	134	55	700	32	19	76	400	94	40	148	1,000	363

N	O	P	Q	R	S	T	U	V	W	X	Y	Z
2,500	157	601	822	344	999	650	975	238	89	12	36	4

Write your name on this line and use the white space to do your computations.

1. _____

Use the chart and numbers to find the values of the names of friends and family members.

2. _____ = _____
(Friend's Name)

3. _____ = _____
(Family Member's Name)

Scholastic Inc. *Summer Express: Between Grades 5 & 6*

Helping Your Middle Schooler Get Ready: Week 4

These are the skills your middle schooler will be working on this week.

Math
- multiplication with regrouping
- converting numbers: fractions, decimals, and percents
- plotting coordinates

Reading
- researching information
- reading for information

Writing
- proofreading symbols
- summarizing information

Vocabulary
- context clues

Grammar
- homophones

Here are some activities you and your middle schooler might enjoy.

Web Quest Use the Internet to search for a topic that interests you and your child. Pick a hobby, a place you'd like to visit, or a favorite music group. Choose five or six sites you think will have information on your topic. Have your child visit each site briefly and give it a "rating" (great, so-so, not good at all) to indicate how effective and informative the sites were. Ask him or her to use the following criteria to determine the best site: 1) gives facts, not opinions, 2) visually interesting and creative, 3) easy to navigate and find facts.

Plan-a-Day Have your child plan on outing. Select a day that everyone can be together all day—and have him or her plan an itinerary for the entire day. Planning the itinerary means he or she will need a timetable or pre-determined schedule for everything. It should include travel time to and from every place, duration of the event, eating, resting, shopping, and maybe others. Your child should research places to visit that are close by, and are free or within your budget. (You may want to establish a budget in advance.)

Your middle schooler might enjoy reading one of the following books:

The Midwife's Apprentice
by Karen Cushman

The Wish Giver: Three Tales of Coven Tree
by Bill Brittain

*Rachel Carson: Clearing the Way
for Environmental Protection*
(Getting to Know the World's Greatest
Inventors & Scientists)
by Mike Venezia

_____ **'s Incentive Chart: Week 4**
Name

This week, I plan to read _____ minutes each day.

CHART YOUR PROGRESS HERE.

Week 1	Day 1	Day 2	Day 3	Day 4	Day 5
I read for...	minutes	minutes	minutes	minutes	minutes
Put a sticker to show you completed each day's work.					

Congratulations!

Wow! You did a great job this week!

Place sticker here.

Parent or Caregiver's Signature _____

At Home With Homophones

Homophones *are words that have the same pronunciation, but different spellings and different meanings.*

Example: My little brother (ate/eight) all (ate/eight) pieces of candy.

Underline the correct homophone in the following sentences.

1. We need to take a (break, brake) from this strenuous work.

2. The sales clerk wanted to (cell, sell) as many (sell, cell) phones as possible.

3. Ross wants his socks because his (tows, toes) are freezing.

4. Jason is going to (wear, ware) his work boots to work today.

5. The new (principal, principle) asked for a meeting of all the parents.

6. Mother does not want to talk about the (passed, past) events in her life.

7. May I go to the birthday party, (to, too, two)?

8. During the math test, the teacher walked down the (aisle, isle) to the back of the room.

9. Zachary has one favorite (pare, pair, pear) of jeans.

10. (Who's, Whose) brown cell phone is that on the corner of the desk?

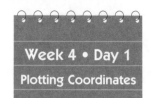

Plotting Coordinates on a Graph

Plot each of the given ordered pairs on the coordinate plane below. Note: Ordered pairs or "*coordinates*" are written with respect to the **x** axis & **y** axis (x, y). See example given.

Amy's Rainfall Record—2011

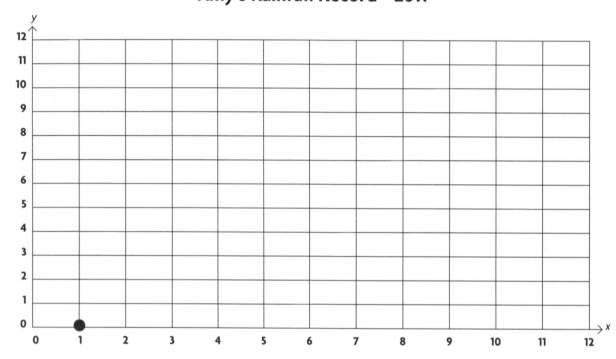

Month of the Year

1. **(1, 0)** ✔

2. **(3, 4)**

3. **(6, 7)**

4. **(8,2)**

5. **(2,1)**

6. **(4,12)**

7. **(5,10)**

8. **(9,3)**

9. **(12,1)**

10. **(7, 2)**

11. **(10, 5)**

12. **(11, 6)**

Scholastic Inc.   *Summer Express: Between Grades 5 & 6*

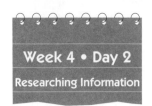

Where in the World?

Where in the world would you find the following cities and geographical features? Research any locations you are not familiar with. Write the country name on the blank.

1. **Rome, Naples, Mount Vesuvius** _____

2. **Nile River, Cairo, Suez Canal** _____

3. **Madrid, Barcelona, Iberian Mountains** _____

4. **Sydney, Great Victoria Desert, Melbourne** _____

5. **Mount Fuji, Hiroshima, Osaka** _____

6. **Cape Town, Johannesburg, Drakensberg Mountains** _____

7. **Paris, Marseille, Alps** _____

8. **Toronto, Rocky Mountains, Victoria Island** _____

9. **Hamburg, Black Forest, Danube River** _____

10. **Casablanca, Atlas Mountains, Rabat** _____

11. **Acapulco, Rio Grande, Baja California** _____

12. **New Delhi, Ganges River, Deccan Plateau** _____

13. **Mount Katahdin, Chicago, San Diego** _____

14. **São Paolo, Amazon Basin, Rio de Janeiro** _____

Using Proofreading Symbols

There are 21 errors in this passage. Read the excerpt. As you find the mistakes, make the appropriate marks to indicate each of the errors. If a change, insertion, or omission is needed, make those changes as well.

Symbol	Explanation
≡	Capitalize a letter
/	Lowercase a letter
⊙	Add a period
⋏	Add a comma
ℯ	Delete a word or a punctuation mark
∧	Insert a word or a punctuation mark
sp	Correct spelling
¶	Begin a new paragraph

Yoga Partners

Meg, and her mom had been going to a wednesday night yoga class togather for about a year Several of Megs friends and their Moms even choze to join them. It was fun relaxing, and challenging. Meg really loved being with her mom as well as taking care of her own body. Meg's mom Alex was a Nurse and had always encouraged her and, her brother to eat well and to particpate in activities they liked. So far, yoga was Meg's favorite but she still played on her school's tennis team and swam every summer on her her neighborhood swim team.

Every Wednesday about 4:30 Meg and her mom ate a light dinner of soup and her mom's famous cheese-veggie wrap's. their class began at 6:00 and lasted one our. Meg loved the way Yoga made her feel because it stretched and toned her muscles. Most of all, Meg and her mom enjoed the deep breathing and meditative quality that caused them to focus on the present moment

Scholastic Inc. Summer Express: Between Grades 5 & 6

Multiplication Mastery

Find the products for the following multiplication problems.

1. 976
    x 719

2. 328
    x 446

3. 899
    x 719

4. 950
    x 568

5. 493
    x 587

6. 755
    x 582

7. 763
    x 167

8. 665
    x 469

9. 800
    x 983

10. 974
    x 314

11. 681
    x 737

12. 175
    x 465

13. 903
    x 941

14. 670
    x 262

15. 536
    x 329

16. 688
    x 640

Giants of the Earth

Think of your favorite tree. Is it big? Next to a **towering** sequoia, it would probably look tiny. Sequoias are very special trees. They are some of the largest and oldest living things on Earth.

Once, there were many different kinds of sequoias. Now, there are only two kinds left. These are the coastal redwoods and the big trees. The **coastal** redwoods grow near the Pacific Ocean. The coastal redwoods are the tallest trees on Earth. Many are over 300 feet tall. That is as tall as a 30-story building! The area where these trees grow is **nicknamed** "the Land of the Giants."

The big trees, or giant sequoias, do not grow along the coast. They are **located** farther inland, in California. The big trees are much wider and heavier than the coastal redwoods. Think of a giraffe and an elephant. This will give you an idea of the difference between the two kinds of sequoias. The coastal redwoods are the "giraffes." The big trees are the "elephants."

The biggest sequoia of all is a big tree called General Sherman. It is one of the most **massive** living things on Earth. This tree is 275 feet tall. It is not as tall as some of the redwoods, but its trunk is the widest. It is more than 100 feet around. Scientists think it weighs more than 6,000 tons!

Sequoias take a long time to get so big. Humans grow for about 20 years, then they stay the same height. Sequoias keep growing as long as they live, and that can be a long time! Scientists say that General Sherman is between 3,000 and 4,000 years old. Think of everything that tree has seen in its lifetime!

Find each vocabulary word in the selection. The words and sentences around it will help you figure out its meaning. Circle the letter with the best definition of the underlined word.

1. **Next to a <u>towering</u> redwood, most trees look tiny.**
   A. made of metal
   B. angry
   C. very tall
   D. very heavy

2. **The <u>coastal</u> redwoods grow near the Pacific Ocean.**
   A. like a roller coaster
   B. mysterious
   C. to slide down a hill
   D. along the coast

3. **The area where the coastal redwoods grow is <u>nicknamed</u> "the land of the Giants."**
   A. given a name that describes a special feature
   B. figured out a tree's height
   C. decided how much a tree weighs
   D. cut down

4. **The big trees are <u>located</u> inland.**
   A. growing
   B. found in a place
   C. stored
   D. at the shore

5. **The big tree called General Sherman is one of the most <u>massive</u> living things on Earth.**
   A. bossy
   B. enormous
   C. full of lumps
   D. interesting

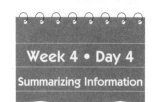

Whales in a Noisy Ocean

Read the article below. Then identify journalism's "5 Ws and 1 H" (Who? What? When? Where? Why? How?) to complete the table with the corresponding information from the article. (There may be more than one answer.) Finally, use your notes to write a 20-word summary.

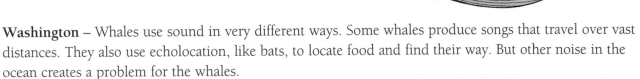

Washington – Whales use sound in very different ways. Some whales produce songs that travel over vast distances. They also use echolocation, like bats, to locate food and find their way. But other noise in the ocean creates a problem for the whales.

Since 1987, the International Fund for Animal Welfare (IFAW) has sent their research vessel *Song of the Whale* around the world to provide a platform for marine research and education. During the travels, the *Song of the Whale* scientists have developed expertise in using underwater microphones to listen to and record the sounds that the animals make. This helps them to track, identify, and survey different species.

One of the threats facing whales and other marine animals is noise pollution in the seas, such as noise from drilling, military activities, oil exploration, and coastal construction. This noise can cause great distress to whales and dolphins and can result in injury and even death.

It is feared this noise pollution may cause mass strandings, when large numbers come ashore and beach together. If the *Song of the Whale* team can track the whales and identify their habitats, then hopefully the nature and location of disturbing noise can be changed.

Who?	
What?	
When?	
Where?	
Why?	
How?	

Write a 20-word summary.

_____

_____

_____

Using a Number Line

Use the first set of number lines to answer questions 1 through 5 below. Then, use what you know about decimals, fractions, percents, and how to convert them to fill in the missing values in the number lines at the bottom of this page.

whole numbers:

0   1   2

fractions:

0   ¼   ½   ¾   1   1¼   1½   1¾   2

decimals:

0   .25   .50   .75   1.0   1.25   1.50   1.75   2.0

percents:

0   25%   50%   75%   100%   125%   150%   175%   200%

1. **What are the fraction and decimal equivalents for 25%?** _____ & _____

2. **What is the decimal equivalent of 125%?** _____

3. **What is the same as ½ when represented as a decimal and percent?** _____ & _____

4. **What decimal amount is twice as much as 50%?** _____

5. **List the decimal and percent equivalents for the value halfway between ¼ and ¾:**

   a) decimal: _____   b) percentage: _____

Fill in the missing fractions:

0   ¼   ½   _____   _____   1¼   _____   _____   2

Fill in the missing decimals

0   _____   _____   1.00   1.25   _____   _____   2

Scholastic Inc. Summer Express: Between Grades 5 & 6

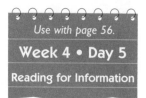

The Arctic: Closer Than You Think

The next time you get caught in a rainstorm, you might have the icy Arctic to thank. It may sound strange, but it's true. This region at the top of the world affects us all. And we affect it!

The Arctic may seem like a foreign land. But scientists say Arctic weather has an impact on weather all over the world. This is how: Cold, dry air forms over the Arctic, and then wind currents shift this cold air to the south. When this cold air hits warm, wet air, storms form. These storms are part of weather patterns that travel around the globe.

The circle drawn shows the Arctic region.

An Unwanted Gift

The Arctic might bring rainstorms to our part of the world. But what we bring to the Arctic can be much worse. Wind and water carry chemicals from factories in the United States and other countries to the Arctic. There the frigid Arctic environment functions like a freezer. Chemicals last for a long time in the atmosphere around the North Pole. These chemicals get into the food supply. The animals and people of the Arctic region can get sick from drinking polluted water. They can get ill from eating polluted food.

Science at the North Pole

Because so much pollution ends up in the Arctic, scientists say it's a good place to study the environment. They examine the icy ocean. They study the nearby land. They test the Arctic air. That gives them an idea of how much pollution the world is creating. It tells them about the health of the whole planet.

Answer the following questions based on the information you read in the passage.
Circle the letter of the correct response.

1. **The center of the Arctic region is at**
   A. the North Pole
   B. the South Pole
   C. Greenland
   D. Alaska

2. **Look at the map. Which of these is not part of the Arctic region?**
   A. Asia
   B. North America
   C. Africa
   D. Europe

3. **Arctic weather affects weather all over the world because**
   A. It is extremely cold.
   B. Arctic winds move south and form storm patterns that travel around the globe.
   C. Arctic air is polluted.
   D. Chemicals last a long time near the North Pole.

4. **Why is the Arctic a good place for scientists to study air and water pollution?**
   A. The Arctic has clean air and water.
   B. Pollution from all over the world collects in the Arctic.
   C. No one bothers the scientists there.
   D. The Arctic Ocean is at the North Pole.

5. **The amount of pollution in the Arctic tells scientists**
   A. How much pollution the world is creating.
   B. That it is too polluted for people to live there.
   C. That people should stop working in factories.
   D. That chemicals will get into the food supply.

6. **Animals and people in the Arctic region can get sick from**
   A. Living in freezing temperatures.
   B. Drinking polluted water.
   C. Experiencing stormy weather patterns.
   D. Testing the air and water.

7. **Why might the Arctic seem like a foreign land?**
   A. It's a great place to go on vacation.
   B. Many people live there.
   C. Scientists study it.
   D. It's very different from where we live.

8. **Look at the map. Which of these cities is a state capital?**
   A. Juneau
   B. Nuuk
   C. Reykjavik
   D. Oslo

Scholastic Inc.   *Summer Express: Between Grades 5 & 6*

Helping Your Middle Schooler Get Ready: Week 5

These are the skills your middle schooler will be working on this week.

Math

- multiplying decimals
- division with remainders
- converting numbers: fractions, decimals, and percents

Reading

- making inferences
- reading for understanding

Writing

- parts of a paragraph

Grammar

- parts of speech
- diagramming sentences
- punctuation: colons and semicolons

Here are some activities you and your middle schooler might enjoy.

Prequel or Sequel? So many movies, stories, and even some television programs show only one part or time of a character's life. Let your child choose a familiar book, movie, or TV show and write, or "storyboard," a *new* plot to extend the story. Telling what happened *before* the original movie/story plot creates a "prequel." If the plot gives a glimpse into the time and experiences *after* the original plot, then it is a "sequel." Movie makers do this often if they have a movie that was a box-office hit. Have your child share the storyboard with other family members.

Learn a Skill—Share a Skill! Is there someone your child admires because this person can do something interesting? What can your child do that someone else might not have tried? Have your middle schooler pick someone he or she knows who has a "cool" craft or skill that he or she would like to learn and give that person a call. Your child might just get a free lesson! Then, have your child consider sharing one of his or her talents with someone younger. Check with that child's parents first, of course.

Your middle schooler might enjoy reading one of the following books:

Guide to the Planet
by Matthew Murrie and Steve Murrie

The Truth About Sparrows
by Marian Hale

Secret Identity Crisis
(The Amazing Adventures of Nate Banks)
by Jake Bell

_____'s Incentive Chart: Week 5

Name

This week, I plan to read _____ minutes each day.

CHART YOUR PROGRESS HERE.

Week 1	Day 1	Day 2	Day 3	Day 4	Day 5
I read for...	minutes	minutes	minutes	minutes	minutes
Put a sticker to show you completed each day's work.					

Congratulations!

Wow! You did a great job this week!

Place sticker here.

 Parent or Caregiver's Signature _____

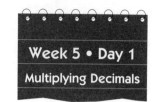
Multiplying Decimals

Review the rules for multiplying decimals. Then solve the problems.

Rules

1. *Multiply as you would whole numbers.*
2. *The number of decimal places in the product is the sum of the decimal places in the factors.*

Remember: *When you see a problem presented horizontally, line up the numbers on the right. Do **not** line up the decimal points.*

Example:

Factor	.4	1 decimal place
Factor	x .9	1 decimal place
Product	.36	2 decimal places

.35 x 0.8 =

Correct	Incorrect
.35	.35
x 0.8	x 0.8

1.　.6
　　x .4

2.　9.4
　　x 7.6

3.　3.1
　　x 6.3

4.　2.9
　　x 1.5

5.　6.8
　　x 0.35

6.　9.27
　　x 6.6

7.　2.2
　　x 9.49

8.　5.99
　　x 5.6

9.　4.8
　　x 7.7

10.　5.6
　　x 7.6

11.　2.9
　　x 6.15

12.　8.6
　　x 5.8

13.　2.23
　　x 0.337

14.　1.6
　　x 0.797

15.　0.72
　　x 5.79

16.　7.71
　　x 0.226

Know Your Word Types

In each sentence, decide whether the underlined word is a **noun** (N), **pronoun** (PN), **verb** (V), **adjective** (ADJ), **adverb** (ADV), **conjunction** (C), **preposition** (P), or **interjection** (I). Then write its abbreviation on the line before the sentence.

_____ 1. What is the world's most widely spoken <u>language</u>?

_____ 2. My soda <u>can</u> was extremely cold when I drank it.

_____ 3. That large, <u>extravagant</u> home is overpriced for this neighborhood.

_____ 4. What is the <u>difference</u> between a hurricane and a storm?

_____ 5. <u>Oh!</u> I know how to complete that science experiment.

_____ 6. <u>She</u> also enjoys cooking chicken dishes and delicious desserts.

_____ 7. The <u>dusty</u> staircase in the old house made my aunt sneeze.

_____ 8. <u>Dusty</u> is our favorite horse on my grandfather's farm.

_____ 9. <u>Hippos</u> may look cute, but they are actually quite dangerous.

_____ 10. My dad is not a great singer, <u>but</u> I love him anyway.

_____ 11. When the phone <u>rings</u>, my sister runs to answer it.

_____ 12. The lady wore several <u>rings</u> on both of her hands.

_____ 13. The students sat <u>quietly</u> and listened to the teacher.

_____ 14. Sarah's puppy jumped <u>over</u> the bush and ran through the neighbor's garden.

_____ 15. <u>Slowly</u> the conductor directed his orchestra through the ballad.

_____ 16. Many <u>restaurants</u> serve salads with every entrée.

Scholastic Inc.   Summer Express: Between Grades 5 & 6

Divide & See What Remains

Find the quotients for the following division problems. Be sure to include the remainders in your answer.

1. $45\overline{)93}$

2. $15\overline{)934}$

3. $17\overline{)206}$

4. $13\overline{)27}$

5. $33\overline{)87}$

6. $82\overline{)86}$

7. $7\overline{)90}$

8. $2\overline{)77}$

9. $13\overline{)79}$

10. $14.7\overline{)139}$

11. $7\overline{)708}$

12. $23\overline{)407}$

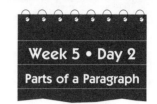

Create a Paragraph

A **paragraph** *is a group of sentences that tells about one main idea.*

The **topic sentence** *tells the main idea and is usually the first sentence.*

Supporting sentences *tell more about the main idea.*

The **closing sentence** *of a paragraph often retells the main idea in a different way.*

Some paragraphs also have a **title***.*

Here are the parts for one paragraph:

Paragraph Title	*Our Summer Vacation*
Topic Sentence	*The first day of our vacation was very disappointing.*
Supporting Sentences:	*1. It rained non-stop from sunrise to sunset.*
	2. Thunder and lightning occurred all day long, so we had to stay indoors.
	3. The second day, we gladly went to the beach.
	4. The sky was blue, and the sun shone brightly.
	5. We built sand castles, went swimming and surfing.
Closing Sentence	*The weather was perfect the rest of the week. I'm so glad I didn't go home after the first day!*

When you write a paragraph, remember the following rules:

• **Indent** *the first line so that readers know that you are beginning a paragraph.*

• **Capitalize** *the first word of each sentence.*

• **Punctuate** *each sentence correctly (. , ? !).*

Using all of the information above, rewrite the paragraph. Be sure to follow the rules.

_____

paragraph title

_____

_____

_____

_____

_____

Working With Fractions, Decimals & Percents

Reduce these fractions to lowest terms. Circle the letter with the correct answer.

1. $\frac{9}{21}$ =

   A. $\frac{4}{10}$ B. $\frac{3}{8}$ C. $\frac{3}{7}$ D. $\frac{3}{12}$

2. $\frac{10}{18}$ =

   A. $\frac{5}{9}$ B. $\frac{2}{8}$ C. $\frac{5}{8}$ D. $\frac{2}{3}$

3. $\frac{11}{33}$ =

   A. $\frac{1}{5}$ B. $\frac{2}{11}$ C. $\frac{2}{3}$ D. $\frac{1}{3}$

4. $\frac{13}{39}$ =

   A. $\frac{1}{3}$ B. $\frac{1}{13}$ C. $\frac{4}{13}$ D. $\frac{7}{20}$

Compute the sums and differences of these decimals. Circle the letter with the correct answer.

5. **0.025 + 2.5 =**

   A. 2.552   B. 2.525   C. 2.535   D. 5.025

6. **5.1 + 0.384 =**

   A. 5.484   B. 5.44   C. 5.448   D. 5.584

7. **1 − 0.236 =**

   A. 0.1236   B. 0.00764   C. 1.746   D. 0.764

8. **7.444 + 3.666 =**

   A. 11.11   B. 111.11   C. 1.744   D. 10.11

Convert these decimals and fractions to percents. Circle the letter with the correct answer.

9. **0.25 =**

   A. 0.025%   B. 2.5%   C. 25%   D. 0.25%

10. **0.33 =**

   A. 33%   B. .033%   C. 3.30%   D. 330%

11. $\frac{1}{4}$ =

   A. 2.5%   B. 25%   C. 0.025%   D. 0.25%

12. $\frac{3}{4}$ =

   A. 75%   B. 750%   C. 7.5%   D. 0.75%

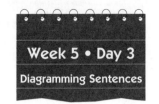

A Picture of the Sentence

To diagram a sentence, first draw a long horizontal line. Then draw a short vertical line that crosses the horizontal line. Write the simple subject to the left of the vertical line. Write the simple predicate to the right of the vertical line. When diagramming sentences, use capital letters as they appear in the sentence, but do **not** use punctuation. *Diagramming a sentence is creating a picture of the sentence.*

Write only the **simple subject** and the **simple predicate** in the diagram.
Remember: The simple predicate can include a helping verb.

Example: The dynamite will explode on schedule.

dynamite	will explode

Diagram only the simple subject and the simple predicate for each of the following sentences.

1. **Rodney went to the library.**

2. **Marsh threw the football.**

3. **Today's special is baked tilapia.**

4. **The heavy rainfall soaked the garden.**

In a sentence diagram, the **direct object** is placed to the right of the simple predicate. The vertical line before the direct object meets but does not cross the horizontal line.

Example: The library needs volunteers.

library	needs	volunteers

Diagram the simple subject, predicate, and direct object.

5. **Fillipe finished the pizza.**

6. **Aunt Jenny bought the tickets.**

Scholastic Inc.   Summer Express: Between Grades 5 & 6

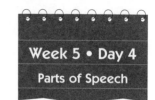

"Going for It"

Do not read the story yet! Give it to a partner and ask him or her to tell you the part of speech under each blank in the story. You say a word for the part of speech, and your partner writes it in the blank. Then your partner reads the story aloud. Now you have created a hilarious story!

It was official! _____ decided to try out for the school soccer team! She _____
           girl's name   **adverb**

wanted to play for the team this _____, but knew the _____ wanted only the
                                         noun   **noun**

_____ players. Therefore, the _____ wouldn't be _____!
adjective ending in "-est"   **noun**   **adjective**

Several _____ passed, and _____ practiced all of her _____
         plural noun   **same girl's name**   **noun**

skills, such as shooting, passing, and _____. Finally, tryout day had _____.
                                     verb ending in "-ing"   **past-tense verb**

She was _____! All the girls were told to run around the _____ for
             adjective   **noun**

_____ minutes. This way the _____ would see the strength of their stamina,
number (more than 1)   **noun**

_____ and _____. Finally, after all of the _____, the coach
   noun   **noun**   **verb ending in "-ing"**

made a _____. The first four _____ the coach called weren't hers. Then, another
            noun   **plural noun**

five were _____, and the next to last _____ was HERS!! She shouted,
         past-tense verb   **noun**

"_____!" and ran over to the _____ to hug her.
  an exclamation   **noun**

What a great _____ !
               noun

Conquering Colons & Semicolons

Use a **semicolon** *to join parts of a compound sentence when a conjunction such as* and, but, *or* or *is not used.*
Example: Marsha likes oatmeal for breakfast; I prefer pancakes.

Use a **colon** *to introduce a list of items that ends a sentence. Words such as* these, the following, *and* as follows *introduce lists.*
Example: For drinks we have the following: milk, juice, water, and soda.

Add semicolons and colons where needed. Write **C** on the line if a sentence or phrase is already punctuated correctly.

_____ 1. **Earth is the third planet from the sun Mars is the fourth.**

_____ 2. **These are my favorite snacks: apples, popcorn, or a slice of cheese.**

_____ 3. **My favorite numbers are as follows: 50, 66, and 88.**

_____ 4. **The movie only cost $5.00 you gave him $10.00.**

_____ 5. **Cuba is a very warm country Canada is much colder.**

_____ 6. **The math test will focus on the following decimals, fractions, and percents.**

_____ 7. **The movie starts at eight o'clock we should be there a few minutes earlier.**

_____ 8. **This is a picture of my mom; my dad is standing behind her.**

_____ 9. **My mother is not home please call back later.**

_____ 10. **We are visiting these states on vacation Maine, Vermont, and New Hampshire.**

_____ 11. **Robby is a good writer he draws well, too.**

_____ 12. **I have three best friends Alex, Tony, and Erik.**

Monopoly on Atlantic City

Atlantic City, N.J.—Times are tough. Jobs are scarce. Money is tight. A lot of people don't have a cent to spend. That's why people are going wild about the new game, Monopoly.

Monopoly lets you live in a make-believe world full of money. Go to Baltic Avenue and put up a new house. Go to Marvin Gardens and buy four new houses there, too. Go to Park Place and buy a new hotel. With Monopoly money, even a poor person can be a tycoon. He or she can become rich and powerful.

Monopoly is the brainchild of Charles Darrow. Darrow is a salesman. He used to come to Atlantic City on holiday. Then hard times began. Darrow lost his job. But he still had his imagination.

With no job, he had lots of free time. He used it to create a game. He called it *Monopoly* because the word means "the complete control of something." Places on the game board are named for streets in Atlantic City. There's New York Avenue, Pennsylvania Avenue, Boardwalk, and all the rest.

At first, Darrow made the game boards himself. But he couldn't make enough. Too many people wanted them. They loved playing Monopoly. It made them feel wealthy and daring, even if just for the moment.

This year, Darrow sold his game. Now it will be made by a company named Parker Brothers. Let's hope they can make enough!

Based on what you've read, circle the letter with the best answer for each question.

1. **People loved playing Monopoly because**
   A. it let them pretend they had money.
   B. the game was long and boring.
   C. it was about a place for vacations.
   D. the game cost a lot of money.

2. **Why was it unusual for people to be buying houses and hotels in 1935?**
   A. There was nothing for sale.
   B. There was no land to build on.
   C. Atlantic City didn't exist.
   D. People didn't have money to spend.

3. **Why was Monopoly so popular back in 1935?**
   A. People were tired of the same old games.
   B. Atlantic City was a popular vacation spot.
   C. Many people were poor then but they could play at being a rich tycoon.
   D. They wanted to have a board game made by Charles Darrow.

4. **Where did the names Park Place and Marvin Gardens come from?**
   A. They are places found in Atlantic City.
   B. They do not exist anywhere.
   C. They are places in Darrow's hometown.
   D. They are names found in many cities.

5. **Why did Charles Darrow sell his game to Parker Brothers?**
   A. He couldn't make enough game boards.
   B. The company loved playing the game.
   C. He had to move to another city.
   D. He wanted to invent a new game.

6. **Why was the game named Monopoly?**
   A. Charles Darrow probably wanted complete control of it.
   B. The object of the game was to own everything.
   C. Charles Darrow was rich.
   D. Darrow did not like to play games.

The Farm

Mark loved visiting his grandfather's farm. He loved his lone walks over the freshly plowed soil that seemed to be patiently waiting for the next planting season. The new season would arrive soon and, in time, another bounty of corn, cotton, and soybeans would spring forth. Grandfather's work would be justly rewarded again. His life was this farm. It was all he knew, except for baseball. Grandfather was one of seven boys, and they all worked this farm for their father, Walter Baker. The Baker boys were expected to rise before dawn, feed animals, load hay barns, and oil tractors, all before breakfast and departing for school. After school, they had additional chores to tend to once homework and dinner were out of the way.

This was their life, and it was a good one. It provided the Baker family with all they needed for food and finances. It also provided the eight Baker boys with amazing physical strength for playing high school sports and rising to star status in a five-county area. Farm work was physical; it was hard and it was not usually done very fast. This meant strength, discipline, stamina, and focus were all deeply engrained in these young men, and their high school coaches loved it.

Mark's grandfather was the baseball star, while his seven brothers mostly pursued football, track, and basketball. They all were offered college scholarships. They all graduated with business or agriculture degrees, but they all returned to Airedale County as that was what they knew, and the majors meant too much travel and separation from family. That was not the Baker family style back then.

February was approaching and that meant decision time was getting close for Mark. Mark spent a great deal of time at the farm with Grandfather over the Christmas holidays. They spent hours talking about baseball, of course, but also about Mark's choices for college or professional baseball. Only two weeks earlier Mark received a call from a scout for the Arizona Diamondbacks telling him of their interest in the upcoming draft. Mark was flabbergasted. He was giddy with the whole idea of being a professional baseball player and knew that if Arizona was looking at him, other teams would soon follow. This complicated his decision making, but he knew with Grandfather's wisdom and Baker family values, the ultimate decision would be one he would never regret. Life as a Baker boy playing baseball would be great no matter what field it would be on. And after baseball, there was another field waiting for him, too, ready for a planting.

Use the story to answer the following questions. Use an additional sheet of paper if needed.

1. **Describe Mark's grandfather.** _____

_____

2. **What sport is shared by the boy and the grandfather?** _____

3. **How did life on the farm help Mark's grandfather?** _____

_____

4. **Who is living in Airedale during the setting of this story?** _____

5. **What decision is Mark facing?** _____

Scholastic Inc.   Summer Express: Between Grades 5 & 6

These are the skills your middle schooler will be working on this week.

Math
- basic operations
- measurement and capacity
- geometric concepts
- measuring volume
- fraction word problems

Reading
- understanding topic sentences

Writing
- thank-you letter
- research skills

Vocabulary
- tricky words

Spelling
- parts of speech

Here are some activities you and your middle schooler might enjoy.

Invent Something Encourage your child to be an inventor! Let him or her use items you would ordinarily discard (e.g., empty containers, lone parts of a game, unusable objects, etc.) to invent a special device. Maybe it will do an ordinary task in a new way or bring people enjoyment. Rube Goldberg is a well-known inventor who creates some zany, overcomplicated inventions that do ordinary tasks. Check out some of his contraptions online for ideas.

Clean Sweep Together with your child, gather up items you no longer need that have been hiding in your closets. Search for books, CDs, old electronics, and even some gently worn clothing. Once you have gathered these forgotten treasures, hold a "Dollar" yard sale, pricing everything super cheap—from $1 to $3 dollars *only*. Or, find a local merchant who pays cash for "gently used junk" or items like yours. Many consignment shops even pay cash on the spot! You'll have a cleaner closet and some money in your pocket!

Your middle schooler might enjoy reading one of the following books:

The Westing Game
by Ellen Raskin

Tuck Everlasting
by Natalie Babbitt

Under the Blood-Red Sun
by Graham Salisbury

_____'s Incentive Chart: Week 6
Name

This week, I plan to read _____ minutes each day.

CHART YOUR PROGRESS HERE.

Week 1 I read for...	Day 1	Day 2	Day 3	Day 4	Day 5
	minutes	minutes	minutes	minutes	minutes
Put a sticker to show you completed each day's work.					

Congratulations!

Wow! You did a great job this week!

Place sticker here.

Parent or Caregiver's Signature _____

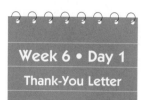
A Puzzling Letter

Rewrite the thank-you letter below. Correct the errors in subject-verb agreement, sentence fragments, run-on sentences, spelling, capitalization, and punctuation. Always indent each new paragraph.

dear aunt Helen and uncle george since we returned home. I have been thinking what a great time we had visiting you in Jackson hole Wyoming. Perhaps my most fond memory were visiting the grand teton mountains riding those beautifull horses near Jenny lake was Jason's favorite activity? Waking up every morning to a home-cooked breakfast was such a treat for me hiking up the mountain near your home was exhausting but great exercise! we have been compileing our picture album when we finish, we want to show our friends what a fun vacation we had with you. As soon as Jason has made the final picture selections, he will email you some of the pictures. Thanks so much for such an enjoyable week in Wyoming.
Love, Jennifer

_____

_____

_____

_____

_____

_____

_____

_____

_____

_____

_____

_____

_____

_____

Reviewing the Basics

Solve the following problems. Be sure to watch the operations signs.
Show any remainders as fractions.

1.   2,498
     + 3,501

2.   8,905
      - 755

3.   1,987
     + 2,391

4.   7,533
     - 3,474

5.   6,664
      + 588

6.   72,819
     + 39,491

7.   16,528
      - 8,263

8.   729
     x 44

9.   5,555
     x 47

10.   8,904
      - 135

11.   1,527
     x 349

12. $871 \times 415 =$

13. $47 \times 504 =$

14. $783 \div 3 =$

15. $387 \div 8 =$

16. $62 \times 35 =$

17. $2,222 \div 11 =$

18. $9 \times 888 =$

19. $1,862 \div 38 =$

20. $60 \overline{)5,040}$

Scholastic Inc. Summer Express: Between Grades 5 & 6

Measuring Up

Convert each measurement. Use a calculator to check for accuracy.

> 12 inches (in.) = 1 foot (ft)   3 ft = 1 yard (yd)

1. **12 in.** = _____ **ft**
2. **1 yd** = _____ **in.**
3. **8 ft** = _____ **in.**

4. **24 ft** = _____ **yd**
5. **81 ft** = _____ **yd**
6. **12 yd** = _____ **ft**

7. **42 ft** = _____ **yd**
8. **11 ft** = _____ **in.**
9. **120 in.** = _____ **ft**

> 1 kilometer (km) = 1,000 meters (m)   10 dm = 100 centimeters (cm)
> 1 m = 10 decimeters (dm)   100 cm = 1,000 millimeters (mm)

10. **8 cm** = _____ **m**
11. **15 km** = _____ **m**
12. **900 dm** = _____ **cm**

13. **848 m** = _____ **km**
14. **45 dm** = _____ **m**
15. **100 dm** = _____ **mm**

16. **45 m** = _____ **dm**
17. **50 km** = _____ **dm**
18. **9 m** = _____ **cm**

> Metric units of weight are **milligrams** (mg), **grams** (g), and **kilograms** (kg).
>
> 63 kg = _____ g   32 mg = _____ g   1 g   = 1000 mg
> 1 kg = 1000 g   1 mg = 0.001 g   1 kg = 1000 g
> 63 kg = (63 x 1000) g   32 mg = (32 x 0.001) g   1 mg = 0.001 g
> 63 kg = 63,000 g   32 mg = 0.032 g   1 g   = 0.001 kg

19. **2000 mg** = _____ **g**
20. **4 kg** = _____ **g**

21. **250 mg** = _____ **kg**
22. **90 g** = _____ **mg**

23. **1500 mg** = _____ **g**
24. **18 g** = _____ **mg**

Commonly Confused Words

Some words are often mixed up or misused because they sound similar, even though they have different spellings and meanings. Underline the correct word that best completes each sentence.

1. Tony's cousins offered to show him (their, there) secret clubhouse.

2. Please (sit, set) down, Jennifer.

3. (Lay, Lie) the newspapers on the top of the cabinet.

4. Marcus took pictures of his trip through the (desert, dessert).

5. Beth will (right, write) a letter to her friend in Chile.

6. Please remember to bring (your, you're) camera.

7. The bright sun cast (it's, its) rays across the valley.

8. Mom's cat might (brake, break) that priceless vase.

9. How could you possibly (lose, loose) such a large coat?

10. Mrs. Denman (accepted, excepted) Jose's late project.

11. The rainstorm had very little (affect, effect) on the hikers.

12. Carmen, please (leave, let) me go with you to the grocery store.

13. The sun will (rise, raise) in the East.

14. Kathryn borrowed (for, four) videos from Phyllis.

15. Dividing fractions was today's math (lessen, lesson).

16. The luxury ship's captain had gone off the designated (coarse, course).

Scholastic Inc.   Summer Express: Between Grades 5 & 6

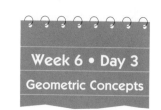
Geometry Review

Use what you already know about geometry and geometrical vocabulary to answer the following questions.

1. **If a rectangle is 15 inches long, and 8 inches wide, what is its surface area?**

    A. 125 sq in.   B. 120 sq in.   C. 130 sq in.   D. 135 sq in.

2. **What is the perimeter of an 8-inch square?**

    A. 32 inches   B. 64 inches   C. 16 inches   D. 24 inches

3. **What is the geometrical term for the line that bisects a circle?**

    A. radius   B. circumference   C. area   D. diameter

4. **If you need to calculate the volume of a solid figure, the measurement is reported in:**

    A. square units   B. cubic units   C. standard units   D. inches

5. **Volume is calculated in rectangular forms by using this formula: *l* x *w* x *h*.
    What do these letters represent in the formula?**

    A. length, weight, and height   C. latitude, width, and heat
    B. length, width, and height   D. longitude, width, and height

6. **What is half of a circle's diameter called?** _____

7. **A cube has a known side measurement of 4 inches long. Is it possible to find the cube's volume without any more information? Explain your answer.**

    _____

    _____

    _____

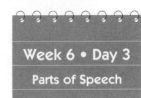

Create Your Own Cartoon

The chart below includes robust vocabulary for some of the most common parts of speech. It also includes the poetic device **onomatopoeia**. Onomatopoeia is use of a word that sounds just like what it is. These words are often used in cartoons to emphasize actions or provide descriptions.

Noun	Verbs	Adjectives	Prepositions	Onomatopoeia
blog	blogging	atomic	over	pop
mall	shred	unreal	under	swoosh
cell phone	bolt	righteous	between	boom
mom	disappear	awesome	about	cuckoo

Use some of these suggestions or come up with your own to create a newspaper cartoon. The frames below are ready for your story and graphics. Draw speech and thought bubbles for your characters' dialogue. Many authors begin with pictures, while others start with a story. Do what works best for you. Remember: Be brief yet interesting; that's what makes a good cartoon.

(Name of Cartoon)

Scholastic Inc. Summer Express: Between Grades 5 & 6

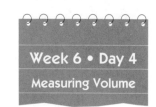

Not All Volume Is Loud . . .

The problems on this page deal with measuring the volume of solid figures. Formulas for finding the volume of solid figures are listed in the box below. Refer to them as needed while you work.

Formulas

Rectangular prism	$V = l \times w \times h$
Rectangular pyramid	$V = \frac{1}{3} (l \times w \times h)$
Cylinder	$V = \Pi \times r^2 \times h$
Cone	$V = \frac{1}{3} (\Pi \times r^2 \times h)$

1. **Choose the solid figure with a volume you can determine using this formula:**
   $V = \Pi \times r^2 \times h$
   A. cone
   B. cylinder
   C. rectangular pyramid
   D. rectangular prism

2. **What is the volume of a box that is 4 inches wide, 6 inches tall and 8 inches long?**
   A. $V = 192$ in.^{3}
   B. $V = 144$ in.^{3}
   C. $V = 121$ in.^{3}
   D. $V = 84$ in.^{3}

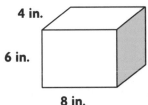

3. **What is the difference in volume of the cubes shown below?**
   A. 729 in.^{3}
   B. 27 in.^{3}
   C. 702 in.^{3}
   D. 360 in.^{3}

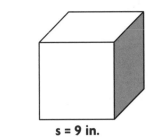

4. **Which formula will correctly figure the volume of a rectangular pyramid?**
   A. $V = l \times w \times h$
   B. $V = \frac{1}{3} (l \times w \times h)$
   C. $V = \frac{1}{3} (\Pi \times r^2 \times h)$
   D. $V = 3 (l \times w \times h)$

5. **Which formula will find the correct volume of the cylinder pictured at right?**
   A. $V = (3.14 \times 5^2 \times 10)$
   B. $V = (3.14 \times 25 \times 10)$
   C. $V = (3.14 \times 2.5^2 \times 10)$
   D. $V = (3.14 \times 44 \times 5)$

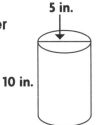

5 in.

10 in.

6. **If a child's sandbox measures 28 inches long, 36 inches wide, and 8 inches high, the volume of sand it will hold is:**
   A. 72 in.^{3}
   B. 8,064 in.^{3}
   C. 864 in.^{3}
   D. 644 in.^{3}

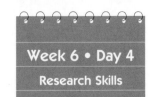

Electronic Reference Sources

Challenge a friend or family member to answer the following Science Trivia questions, or do this exercise by using the Internet, an online encyclopedia, or trustworthy database site.

1. **How many minutes does it take the average person to fall asleep?** _____

2. **What is the largest venomous snake?** _____

3. **What is the human bone most frequently broken?** _____

4. **Do mosquitoes have teeth?** _____

5. **What is the base unit of mass in the metric system?** _____

6. **What is the little ridge between your nose and upper lip called?** _____

7. **What is the opening at the top of a volcano called?** _____

8. **What computer was introduced in the 1984 Super Bowl ads?** _____

9. **How many calories are in a glass of water?** _____

10. **What is the most common blood type?** _____

11. **What is the fastest reptile on land?** _____

12. **What method of underwater detection is short for "sound navigation and ranging"?** _____

13. **What substance earns recyclers the most money?** _____

14. **What planet is the brightest object in the sky after the sun and moon?** _____

15. **What liquid metal was commonly used in thermometers?** _____

Scholastic Inc.   Summer Express: Between Grades 5 & 6

Fraction Fun

Solve each fraction word problem. Then circle the best answer. Be sure to show your work.

1. Ryan has $17\frac{3}{8}$ yards of coated wire for his zip line. He used $8\frac{1}{4}$ yards to section off the ride area between 2 trees. How many yards of wire does he have left?

   A. $7\frac{5}{8}$ B. $9\frac{1}{8}$ C. $10\frac{1}{8}$ D. $21\frac{5}{8}$

2. It takes 4 hours to clean the Eubanks' condo. How many hours does it take to clean $\frac{7}{8}$ of it?

   A. $3\frac{1}{2}$ B. $3\frac{3}{4}$ C. $2\frac{4}{9}$ D. $3\frac{1}{8}$

3. Mr. Palter purchased 30 blank rewritable CDs. He placed $\frac{1}{5}$ of the CDs in his briefcase. How many CDs did Mr. Palter pack in his briefcase?

   A. 5   B. 12   C. 6   D. 60

4. Maria made 3 dresses for the Greek Festival dance. She used $6\frac{3}{8}$ yards of fabric for all 3 dresses. If she adds $2\frac{3}{8}$ yards of trim to the dresses, how many total yards of material will she use?

   A. $10\frac{1}{4}$ B. $9\frac{3}{8}$ C. $7\frac{5}{8}$ D. $9\frac{3}{4}$

5. John has $\frac{1}{2}$ of a pizza left in the fridge. For breakfast he ate $\frac{1}{3}$ of it. What fraction of that does he have left?

   A. $\frac{5}{6}$ B. $\frac{2}{3}$ C. $\frac{2}{5}$ D. $\frac{1}{6}$

6. The 8th grade orchestra performed 3 songs at the concert. The first song was $3\frac{3}{4}$ minutes long. The next song was $5\frac{1}{4}$ minutes long. The last song was $4\frac{1}{2}$ minutes. How many minutes did the orchestra play in all?

   A. $13\frac{1}{2}$ B. $12\frac{3}{4}$ C. $11\frac{1}{4}$ D. $14\frac{1}{2}$

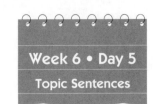

Creating a Topic Sentence

Commonly appearing at (or near) the beginning of a paragraph, a **topic sentence** expresses the main idea of the paragraph. What usually follows are sentences that develop the main idea with specific details. Using the information given in each paragraph below, create a topic sentence that will interest readers, then write it on the line provided.

1. Mount Everest is 29,079 feet (8,863 meters) above sea level. It is part of the Himalayan range in South Asia. Despite its awesome height, the mountain has been climbed many times. Sir Edmund Hillary and his guide, Tenzing Norgay, were the first to climb the mountain, reaching the summit on May 29, 1953. Mount Everest attracts well-experienced mountaineers as well as novice climbers who are willing to pay substantial sums to professional mountain guides to complete a successful climb.

_____

2. Harriet Tubman was an African-American spy for the Union Army during the American Civil War. After escaping from slavery, into which she was born, Tubman made 13 missions, rescuing over 70 slaves, via a network of antislavery activists and safe houses known as the Underground Railroad. She traveled by night in extreme secrecy. Harriet (or "Moses," as she was called) never lost a passenger. Large rewards were offered for the capture and return of many of the people she helped escape; however, no one ever knew it was Harriet Tubman who was helping them.

_____

3. Alligators and crocodiles have been considered villainous, man-eating monsters for centuries, but this was not always the case. Many tall tales have been told about these giant reptiles with long tails. This is partly due to the fact that crocodiles and alligators have truly ancient roots, going all the way back to when dinosaurs still roamed the earth. The two reptiles are often confused, but visually crocodiles and alligators are quite different. Alligators have a very broad, wide snout, and crocodiles have a narrower snout and jaw.

_____

4. Hoover Dam, once known as Boulder Dam, is a concrete, arch-gravity dam in the Black Canyon of the Colorado River. The dam is located on the border between Arizona and Nevada. It was constructed between 1931 and 1936 and dedicated on September 30, 1935 by President Franklin Roosevelt. The dam is 726 feet high and 1,244 feet wide. Hoover Dam was actually built to help the farmers in Arizona, Nevada, and southern California. For years, the farmers were flooded once a year. The dam was built to stop the floods and also provide electricity for Arizona, Nevada, and part of California.

_____

Scholastic Inc.   Summer Express: Between Grades 5 & 6

Helping Your Middle Schooler Get Ready: Week 7

These are the skills your middle schooler will be working on this week.

Math
- Roman numerals
- converting numbers: fractions, decimals, and percents
- plane figures and symmetry
- interpreting a bar graph

Reading
- main idea

Writing
- persuasive writing
- sequencing

Vocabulary
- dictionary skills
- alphabetical order

Grammar
- pronouns
- subject-verb agreement

Here are some activities you and your middle schooler might enjoy.

Folks, That's a Wrap! Everyone uses gift wrap, greeting cards, or stationery. Consider making some of your own using things you may not ordinarily think of when you think "gift wrap" or "greeting cards." Together with your child, make some unusual gift wrap that puts the rolled wrapping paper back in the closet! Use an old t-shirt you don't wear anymore but that has cool designs on it. Perhaps some torn pants could serve as gift covering, and the back pocket could be the "envelope" for your custom-made card. Most re-purposed items do not even need any sewing as long as you have other materials like hot glue, fabric glue, staples, etc.

Roam for Roman Numerals

Why not go for a walk together in your neighborhood with pen and paper? Encourage your child to look for numbers everywhere and write them down. Have him or her compile a list of all numbers you see—house numbers, license plate

numbers, mailbox numbers—wherever you see them. When you return home have your child write each number in Roman numerals. Perhaps your child could challenge you to do some conversions, too!

Your middle schooler might enjoy reading one of the following books:

Island of the Blue Dolphins
by Scott O'Dell

Eleven
by Patricia Reilly Giff

Eats, Shoots & Leaves: Why, Commas Really Do Make a Difference!
by Lynne Truss

_____ **'s Incentive Chart: Week 7**
Name

This week, I plan to read _____ minutes each day.

CHART YOUR PROGRESS HERE.

Week 1 I read for...	Day 1 minutes	Day 2 minutes	Day 3 minutes	Day 4 minutes	Day 5 minutes
Put a sticker to show you completed each day's work.					

Congratulations!

Wow! You did a great job this week!

Place sticker here.

Parent or Caregiver's Signature_____

Letter to the Editor

Below is a letter to the editor from a reader who wanted to share a difference of opinion. The letter contains sentences that give strong reasons and valid attempts at persuading the reader to change his or her beliefs. There are also some weak sentences that would not compel a reader to change his or her opinion. On the lines below, list the sentences you find most persuasive.

Dear Editor:

I am writing about an article entitled "Sidewalk Success," which appeared in the January 27th edition of *The Sun Valley Times.* Your reporter described our city's current "operation sidewalk" project as a gift to all of the citizens and stated it would begin in February. It is now March, and nothing is being done to begin this project. There have even been television reports stating the funds are not able to completely cover the cost of the project. I believe you should print a corrected version of this sidewalk story to properly report on the true details of this project.

First, a gift is transferred to another person at no cost to the one receiving it; so these sidewalks are not "gifts." Also, the project needs more time to be done. Proper sidewalk construction takes two weeks to complete, but your reporter stated the entire project will only require ten weeks for nine sidewalks. That is mathematically impossible. Additionally, the project is targeted to help schools and shopping centers, but your reporter did not mention that at all.

There are no flowerbeds at the entrances of Mill Glenn Drive, Applegate Road, and Tilly Pond Street because these areas are waiting for sidewalks. Your reporter did not seem to care about the speed of this project and how a quick and efficient process would help everyone. I would appreciate it if your staff would consider reporting on this project again, and in a truthful and complete manner for the citizens of our town.

Best regards,

Tim W.
Sun Valley, Idaho

On the lines below, list the points you believe the writer makes in this letter that are most persuasive.

_____

_____

_____

_____

_____

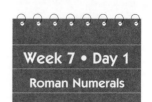

Roman Numerals—As Easy as I, II, III

Convert the numbers. The first one has been done for you.

| I = 1 | V = 5 | X = 10 | L = 50 | C = 100 | D = 500 | M = 1,000 |

1. **DCCCXLII =**

    _____842_____

2. **MDCXI =**

    _____

3. **MDCXLVIII =**

    _____

4. **1698 =**

    _____

5. **MMCLXXIV =**

    _____

6. **CMLXIX =**

    _____

7. **MCCCXVII =**

    _____

8. **62 =**

    _____

9. **MCDXL =**

    _____

10. **MMDCCCLXX =**

    _____

11. **882 =**

    _____

12. **DXXXIV =**

    _____

13. **993 =**

    _____

14. **MMCDLXXXIX =**

    _____

15. **DCLIII =**

    _____

Complete the following addition and subtraction problems. The first one has been done for you.

16. **LVI + V =**

    _____61, LXI_____

17. **XLV – VIII =**

    _____

18. **LXXIV + LXII =**

    _____

Scholastic Inc.   Summer Express: Between Grades 5 & 6

Identifying the Main Idea

Read the following passage and answer the questions at the bottom of this page.
Pay close attention to the main ideas that are presented in each of the three paragraphs.

The Ming Dynasty

The Ming Dynasty was the ruling dynasty of China from 1368 to 1644. This dynasty, regarded as an era of social stability and orderly government, was the last dynasty in China ruled by the Hans, an ethnic group of Chinese people, perhaps the largest ethnic group in the world. The Ming capital of Beijing fell to a rebellion in 1644, and was succeeded by the Shun and Qing dynasties. The Ming is recognized for its numerous accomplishments, including the establishment of a major navy, an army of one million troops, and flourishing maritime trade. There were enormous construction projects, too, most notably the building of the Great Wall, restoration of the Grand Canal, and creation of the Forbidden City in Beijing.

Because of its many achievements, the Ming Dynasty is considered a high point in Chinese civilization. It is also an era in which the first signs of capitalism emerged in China. The ruling classes as well as people in rural and urban areas experienced great changes—many that were unanticipated and unintended. The great Emperor Hongwu wanted to build a fixed, immobile society of self-sufficient, rural communities that would have no need to interact with urban centers. However, the build-up of China's agricultural base and establishment of strong communication routes due to a militarized courier system had an unintended effect: it created an agricultural surplus, and this supply of goods could be sold at the growing markets all along courier routes. Communication and trade increased and rural regions and commerce were influenced by urban trends.

The upper levels of society, primarily the scholarly-gentry class, were also affected by this new trend toward a consumer culture. Traditionally only the family members of the scholarly class would take the exams to become scholar-officials; but now merchant families offered their own exam candidates and began to assume the cultural practices typical of the gentry. This trend toward change in social class and commercialism was not an isolated one; there were also changes in political and social philosophy, and in arts and literature.

1. **What is the main idea of the first paragraph?** _____

_____

2. **What is the main idea of the second paragraph?** _____

_____

3. **What is the main idea of the third paragraph?** _____

_____

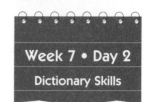

Look It Up!

Match each word with its definition. You may use a dictionary, a science book, or the Internet.

_____ 1. **asteroids**

_____ 2. **crater**

_____ 3. **eclipse**

_____ 4. **igneous**

_____ 5. **meteor**

_____ 6. **planet**

_____ 7. **satellite**

_____ 8. **stratosphere**

_____ 9. **volcano**

_____ 10. **weight**

A. A celestial body that travels in an orbit around a planet or moon

B. The cutting off of light from one celestial body by another

C. A vent in the planetary surface through which magma and associated gases and ash erupt

D. The luminous phenomenon seen when a meteoroid enters the atmosphere, commonly known as a shooting star

E. Any of numerous small, often irregularly shaped bodies that orbit the sun, chiefly in the region of Mars and Jupiter

F. The layer of the earth's atmosphere that lies above the troposphere and below the mesosphere

G. Rock or mineral that solidified from molten or partly molten material

H. A depression formed by the impact of a meteorite, or a depression around the orifice of a volcano

I. The large, spherical body made of rocks and ice orbiting the sun or another star

J. The gravitational force exerted on an object

Write the words in the box below in alphabetical order on the lines provided.

protrude	aggressive	morsel	gorge
sluggish	slither	accommodate	bask
conceal	flail	carcass	ripple

1. _____

2. _____

3. _____

4. _____

5. _____

6. _____

7. _____

8. _____

9. _____

10. _____

11. _____

12. _____

Scholastic Inc.   Summer Express: Between Grades 5 & 6

Shapes in Motion

Look at each pair of figures to decide if they are congruent or similar. Write *similar* or *congruent* below each pair of figures. (To be congruent, the shapes must coincide at all points when one is placed over the other.) Next, find the line or lines of symmetry for each of the figures by drawing a line at each line of symmetry.

1.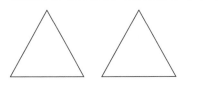

_____

3.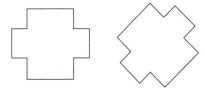

_____

2.

_____

4.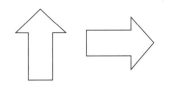

_____

Rotational symmetry: If an object can be rotated a half turn or less around a point and match the original position, then it has *rotational symmetry*.

Example: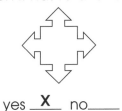

yes __X__ no_____   yes _____ no __X__

Decide if each of the shapes below has rotational symmetry. Mark yes or no.

5.

yes _____ no _____

7.

yes _____ no _____

9.

yes _____ no _____

6.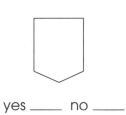

yes _____ no _____

8.

yes _____ no _____

10.

yes _____ no _____

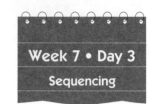

What Happened When?

Read the following e-mail to a friend. Then complete the sequencing activity below.

From	Megan
To	Kat
Subject	Movie Night

Hey Kat!

I know you are busy, but I had to e-mail you about our "movie night." We MISS YOU, kid! You are the one who started "movie night" and well . . . we just miss you! We went to that new movie *Beach Trip* about the three guys who get trapped in a hotel off some weird island near Cancun. Oh, my gosh, it was too awesome! We went to a late movie and didn't get out until after 11:00 p.m. I just knew my parents were going to be all in my business for staying out so late. Actually, they were pretty cool, 'cause I sent them a text when we left about 11:15 p.m. (I guess that helped.) Kyle drove, and I rode in the back with Amy and Jeff. Nate was in the front seat, and he was the last one we had to pick up since he lives so far out. I guess we got to the mall about seven o'clock, then we played some games in that goofy arcade place where all those little kids hang. Ick! We went to that pasta place that makes that amazing pizza and Greek salad. Amy and I HAD to go wash our hands after that slimy, germ-infested arcade! The guys all went to buy the tickets, and we were going to just hang. Then I remembered that PRIMA perfume place you and I LOVE! So, of course, we popped in and had a BLAST! We finally left with, like, 20 samples! Well, it is super late now, and I HAVE to go to this tennis event with my mom in the morning, and she will NOT let me off the hook, so I better go to bed! Oh, I miss you! Have fun up there with your grandparents and COME HOME SOON!

Luv ya!   Megan   ☺

In your own words, write a description of the events Megan describes in her e-mail. Put the events she gives in her account in chronological order of occurrence. Pay close attention to times, activities, and explanations her narrative provides.

_____

_____

_____

_____

_____

Pick Your Pronouns Properly

 A **pronoun** *is a word that is used as a substitute for, or instead of, a noun.*

In each sentence, underline the pronoun that completes each sentence correctly.

Commonly Used Pronouns

Subject: I, you, he, she, it, we, they, who

Object: me, you, him, her, it, us, them, whom

Possessive: my, mine, your, yours, its, her, hers, his, our, ours, their, theirs, whose

1. **(Who, Whose) jacket is on the floor?**

2. **Jamal and (I, me) rode our bicycles to the park to meet friends.**

3. **(We, Us) were all late for the Jackson's dinner party.**

4. **My mother drove Katie and (she, her) to the electronic store.**

5. **(They, Them) mow lawns in the neighborhood in the summer.**

6. **(He, Him) and Cesar will arrive at the concert early.**

7. **Your favorite soccer player is (who, whom)?**

8. **Mark and Brad helped (we, us) carry the grill to the back yard.**

9. **Uncle Oscar told my brothers and (I, me) a ghost story.**

10. **Marcia asked (they, them) to go with her to the play.**

11. **He pushed the shopping cart for (his, him) grandmother.**

12. **Please give the donation to Mr. Smith or (I, me).**

13. **(Who, Whom) are you waiting for?**

14. **Someone has left (his, their) wallet in my car on the back seat.**

15. **(Who, Whom) are the students in the picture in front of the beach house?**

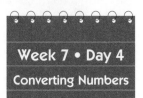
Fractions, Decimals, and Percents

Write each fraction as a percent. Round to the nearest hundredth.
Follow these rules: 1) Change the fraction to a decimal (numerator ÷ denominator).
2) Change the decimal to a percent (multiply by 100). A percent compares a quantity to 100.
If you can make an equivalent fraction with a denominator of 100, then the numerator equals
the percent.

1. $\frac{3}{5}$ _____

3. $\frac{4}{25}$ _____

5. $\frac{17}{25}$ _____

7. $\frac{67}{100}$ _____

2. $\frac{1}{2}$ _____

4. $\frac{22}{100}$ _____

6. $\frac{12}{50}$ _____

8. $\frac{11}{25}$ _____

Write each decimal as a percentage. **Remember:** Decimals that name hundreds can be
written easily as percentages because *percent* means "per hundred."

9. **0.18** _____

11. **0.09** _____

13. **0.35** _____

15. **0.03** _____

10. **0.75** _____

12. **0.54** _____

14. **0.98** _____

16. **0.61** _____

90

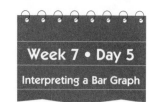

Gridiron Bar Graph

Use the triple bar graph on this page to answer the questions. Some inference and multistep calculations may be needed. Use additional paper if necessary.

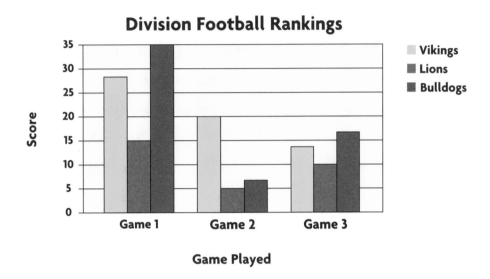

Division Football Rankings

Vikings
Lions
Bulldogs

Score

Game 1   Game 2   Game 3

Game Played

1. **According to the data, which teams had the highest scores in Games 1 and 2?**

_____

2. **Which team(s) did better than the Lions in Game 3?** _____

3. **Which two teams showed the largest drop in score from Game 1 to Game 2?**

_____

4. **Which team(s) had an increase in their score from Game 2 to 3?** _____

5. **Which two games show the greatest difference in score for the Vikings?** _____

6. **What is the difference in the Bulldogs score from Game 2 to 3?** _____

7. **Which team always had a lower score than the other two?** _____

8. **If the trend continues for each of these teams, which team will most likely score highest in the fourth game? Explain.**

_____

Check for Subject-Verb Agreement

Proofread the paragraph for errors in subject-verb agreement. Draw a line through each incorrect verb. Then, on the lines provided below, rewrite the paragraph.

The Henderson High School Orchestra are performing next month at the Decatur Town Square Pavilion. Four dollars are the cost of a ticket for students. A ticket for a non-student are going to cost eight dollars. The orchestra will perform a variety of songs. One song the orchestra will be playing are "Rhapsody in Blue." Members of the audience is being encouraged to sing along with the songs on the program. A portion of the profits from the performance are to be spent on new instruments. Mr. Carson, the orchestra director, were formerly the band director at Tucker High School. The orchestra director are hoping for a large audience at the show. Upon the conclusion of the concert, refreshments is going to be served next door at the Decatur Recreational Center.

_____

_____

_____

_____

_____

_____

_____

_____

_____

Scholastic Inc.   Summer Express: Between Grades 5 & 6

Helping Your Middle Schooler Get Ready: Week 8

These are the skills your middle schooler will be working on this week.

Math
- interpreting a circle graph
- multiplying decimals
- probability

Reading
- reference skills
- reading for details

Writing
- paragraphs using simple tenses

Vocabulary
- word work: synonyms, antonyms, and homophones
- word choice

Grammar
- parts of speech
- verb tenses

Here are some activities you and your middle schooler might enjoy.

People Patrol Suggest that your child invite a friend along to a public place—for instance, a mall, restaurant, park, or other highly populated area. Together, they should watch as many people as possible from a reasonable distance, noticing their clothing and approximate ages. They can use a notepad, electronic device, or fingers to count the types of shoes, pants, shirts, or accessories certain age groups seem to wear most frequently. They may want to limit it to only two age groups and two or three wardrobe items. After about 15 minutes, the friends should discuss their "data collection." This is what market researchers do for a living! Perhaps your child is a marketing genius in the making!

Treasure Not Trash Collage is a well-practiced and popular form of art. It appears in all kinds of media that artists may work in today, including the digital formats. Collage combines color and texture of various items that are often unrelated to each other. Encourage your child to make a self-portrait, a picture of a favorite pet, or a scene using collage as the format. Be kind to the environment, too, and use things that are recyclable. Things that are deemed trash, scrap, and usable refuse make great art for those with a creative goal in mind!

Your middle schooler might enjoy reading one of the following books:

Z Is for Zeus: A Greek Mythology Alphabet
by Helen Wilbur

The Midnight Fox
by Betsy Byars

Savvy
by Ingrid Law

's Incentive Chart: Week 8

This week, I plan to read_____minutes each day.

CHART YOUR PROGRESS HERE.

Week 1	Day 1	Day 2	Day 3	Day 4	Day 5
I read for...	minutes	minutes	minutes	minutes	minutes
Put a sticker to show you completed each day's work.					

Congratulations!

Wow! You did a great job this week!

Place sticker here.

 Parent or Caregiver's Signature_____

Make a Timeline

Use the information in the article to create a bottom tier for the timeline below that tells about the Soviet space program.

The Race for Space

During the 1950s and 1960s, both American and Soviet leaders made space exploration an important goal. Both countries wanted to win the space race to show their scientific superiority and military power.

In 1957, the Soviet Union launched *Sputnik*, the first artificial Earth satellite. Sputnik means "traveler" in Russian. That same year, the Soviets launched *Sputnik II*. The spacecraft carried Laika, a dog, into space.

Two years later, in 1959, the Soviet Union launched *Luna II*, the first space probe to hit the moon. That same year, *Luna III* orbited the moon and took photographs of it.

Yuri Gagarin, a Soviet cosmonaut, became the first person to orbit Earth in 1961. And in 1963, the first woman in space was Soviet cosmonaut Valentina Tereshkova.

The Soviets' accomplishments were impressive and contributed a great deal to what we now know about space.

America's Race to Space

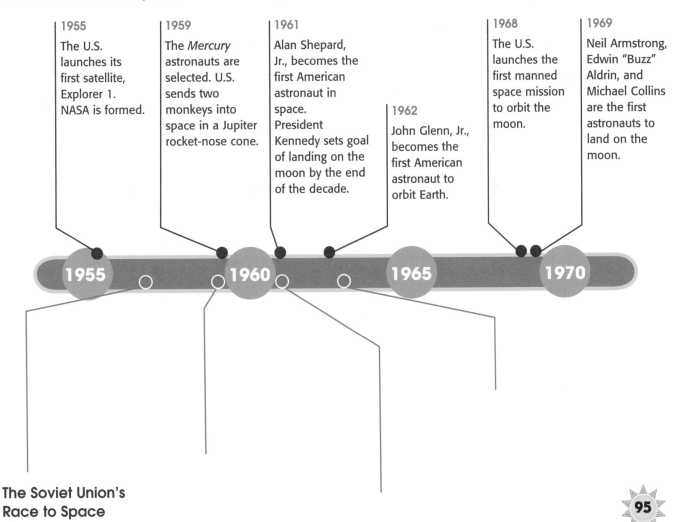

1955
The U.S. launches its first satellite, Explorer 1. NASA is formed.

1959
The *Mercury* astronauts are selected. U.S. sends two monkeys into space in a Jupiter rocket-nose cone.

1961
Alan Shepard, Jr., becomes the first American astronaut in space. President Kennedy sets goal of landing on the moon by the end of the decade.

1962
John Glenn, Jr., becomes the first American astronaut to orbit Earth.

1968
The U.S. launches the first manned space mission to orbit the moon.

1969
Neil Armstrong, Edwin "Buzz" Aldrin, and Michael Collins are the first astronauts to land on the moon.

The Soviet Union's Race to Space

A Piece of the Pie

Study the circle graphs on this page, then answer the following questions by choosing the best answer.

Sadie's Monthly Allowance

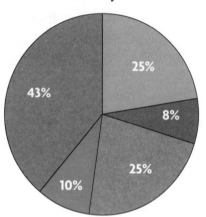

Katie's Monthly Allowance

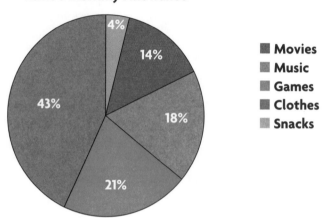

- ■ Movies
- ■ Music
- ■ Games
- ■ Clothes
- ■ Snacks

1. **Which category is the largest expense for Katie and the smallest for Sadie?**
   A. games & clothing
   B. clothing & music
   C. music & snacks
   D. clothing & movies

2. **Katie's chart shows she uses 43% toward clothing. Which category of hers is about 50% of that?**
   A. movies
   B. clothes
   C. music
   D. games

3. **Sadie plans to combine her snacks and movie allocations for two months in order to buy more cool clothes. How much of her allowance will she have to spend on clothing after the two months?**
   A. 65%
   B. 58%
   C. 66%
   D. 56%

4. **If Sadie spends 15% more on games than she does now, what will her total be then?**
   A. 25%
   B. 15%
   C. 10%
   D. 31%

5. **Which two categories does Sadie spend equal amounts on each month, and how do they impact her total monthly allowance distribution?**
   A. She spends equal amounts on clothing and movies and it gives her less for games.
   B. She spends equal amounts on movies and snacks, and it does not affect her budget.
   C. She spends equal amounts on snacks and music and that consumes half of her allowance.
   D. She spends the same as Katie on clothing.

True or False?

Study the definitions of the parts of speech. Write **T** for **true** and **F** for **false**.

_____ 1. **A pronoun takes the place of an adjective.**

_____ 2. **Adjectives describe nouns.**

_____ 3. **A noun is a word that names a person, place, thing, or idea.**

_____ 4. **An adverb can modify another adverb.**

_____ 5. **A preposition begins a prepositional phrase.**

_____ 6. **Interjections are short expressions found at the beginning of a sentence.**

_____ 7. *Or* **is a conjunction.**

_____ 8. **In a sentence, you can have two adjectives in a row.**

_____ 9. *She* **is often considered a preposition.**

_____ 10. **Conjunctions take the place of a noun.**

Identify the underlined word as one of the parts of speech. Circle one of the choices given.

11. <u>Congratulations!</u> You answered the questions correctly.	conjunction	interjection
12. Roger left his gloves <u>on</u> the table.	preposition	adverb
13. Please find the almanac <u>and</u> dictionary on the shelf.	adjective	conjunction
14. Maria had a <u>really</u> great time at the party.	adverb	adjective
15. The <u>Braves</u> won the first game of the season.	adjective	noun
16. Please use the <u>drawing</u> paper in the drawer.	adverb	adjective
17. Are <u>they</u> ever going to arrive?	noun	pronoun
18. Could you <u>possibly</u> help me with this math problem?	adjective	adverb

Using a Table of Contents & Index

Read the Table of Contents and Index. Then answer the questions.

A **table of contents** gives the names of chapters or topics along with page numbers.
An **index** gives the page numbers for more specific information.

1. **In which chapter would you look for information about writing the first draft?**
   A. Chapter 5   C. Chapter 7
   B. Chapter 6   D. Chapter 8

2. **To find out about preparing the bibliography, turn to pages**
   A. 25–30.   C. 31–34.
   B. 77–78.   D. 79–80.

3. **There is some information about polishing the research paper on pages**
   A. 63–76.   C. 95–98.
   B. 35–50.   D. 77–78.

4. **Which chapter would have information on presenting the research paper?**
   A. Chapter 11   C. Chapter 10
   B. Chapter 9   D. Chapter 1

5. **If you wanted to be more specific in choosing your research topic, you would look on pages**
   A. 10–11.   C. 15–21.
   B. 20–21.   D. 107–109.

6. **Where would you look in the index to find information on the Internet?**
   A. pages 20–21   C. pages 52–54
   B. pages 15–21   D. pages 10–11

7. **What page would provide information on how to write the endnotes?**
   A. 18   C. 52
   B. 96   D. 7

8. **If you wanted information on evaluating the final research paper, look on page**
   A. 96.   C. 52.
   B. 107.   D. 97.

Scholastic Inc.   Summer Express: Between Grades 5 & 6

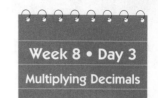

Decimal Practice

Study the example below. Then solve the problems. If necessary, use a separate sheet of paper to do your work.

Rule

1. Multiply as you would whole numbers.
2. The number of decimal places in the product is the sum of the decimal places in the factors.

Remember: when the problem is presented horizontally, line up the numbers on the right. Do **not** line up the decimal points.

Example:

Factor	.6	1 decimal place
Factor	x .7	1 decimal place
Product	.42	2 decimal places

.51 x 0.8 =

	Correct	Incorrect
	.51	.51
	x 0.8	x 0.8

1. .7
    x .8

2. .9
    x .5

3. 2.52
    x 0.5

4. 4.37
    x 0.7

5. 3.69
    x .7

6. .82
    x .15

7. 8.5
    x .27

8. 6.5
    x 8.3

9. **5.47 x 0.5 =**

10. **0.543 x 7.2 =**

11. **0.0082 x 5.36 =**

12. **9.84 x 53.3 =**

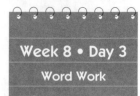

Synonyms, Antonyms & Homophones

Read each statement. Circle the letter next to the correct answer.

1. **Synonyms are words that**
   A. sound the same.
   B. mean almost the same thing.
   C. are spelled the same.
   D. are opposites.

2. **Antonyms are words that**
   A. have almost the same meaning.
   B. always rhyme.
   C. mean the opposite.
   D. sound alike.

3. **Homophones are words that**
   A. sound alike.
   B. mean the opposite.
   C. mean the same thing.
   D. always rhyme.

4. **The words _____ and _____ are antonyms.**
   A. small, tiny
   B. beautiful, lovely
   C. beautiful, careful
   D. beautiful, ugly

5. **The words _____ and _____ are homophones.**
   A. their, there
   B. funny, silly
   C. bunny, money
   D. pretty, ugly

6. **The words _____ and _____ are synonyms.**
   A. small, smile
   B. funny, bunny
   C. tiny, small
   D. tiny, huge

Decide if the two words are **synonyms** or **antonyms**. Write the answer on the line.

7. **illness, sickness** _____

8. **majority, minority** _____

9. **huge, gigantic** _____

10. **blend, combine** _____

11. **increase, decrease** _____

12. **argument, dispute** _____

Underline the correct **homophone** in each sentence. If necessary, use a dictionary.

13. **Corey likes to ride his bike on the scenic (course, coarse) along the Piedmont Park.**

14. **The sergeant was stationed (overseas, oversees) for almost two years.**

15. **Michael recorded the (cereal, serial) numbers of all of his electronic devices.**

16. **My guidance counselor will (council, counsel) me on what subjects to take.**

17. **My brother (ate, eight) all of the ice cream in the freezer.**

18. **All of my brother's (close, clothes) in his closet are clean.**

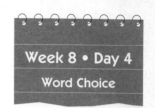

Choose Your Words

Read each sentence below and select the best word to fill in the blank. Be sure to select the word or word phrase that adds the correct emphasis to the sentence. If necessary, use a dictionary or thesaurus for help.

1. **Amanda is the smartest and _____ student in our sixth grade class.**
   A. most discontent
   B. most conscientious
   C. most nicest
   D. most aloof

2. **Warren considers himself an _____ with his new website business.**
   A. entertainer
   B. economist
   C. entrepreneur
   D. elitist

3. **When consumers carefully buy cars, they _____ makes and models very well.**
   A. resurgence
   B. reveal
   C. research
   D. remunerate

4. **Most parents want their kids to succeed and _____ in school as well as in life.**
   A. provide
   B. procure
   C. proper
   D. prosper

5. **For competition, it is _____ that athletes eat right and stay in top physical shape.**
   A. impertinent
   B. imperative
   C. impossible
   D. immunity

6. **Paul and Laura like to shop conservatively, so when they do shop, they are _____.**
   A. frustrated
   B. frivolous
   C. frugal
   D. formative

7. **Sadie likes to travel _____ and, as an international technical consultant, she does.**
   A. enormously
   B. excitedly
   C. extensively
   D. eternally

8. **Billy and Benjamin, who are identical twins, often sing _____.**
   A. duals
   B. duets
   C. duty
   D. deter

9. **Katie and Brianna have many baseball collectibles that are rather _____.**
   A. vulnerable
   B. veneers
   C. valuable
   D. vaulted

10. **Dad decided to vote for the candidate with the best _____.**
    A. reputation
    B. remedies
    C. renaissance
    D. reputed

Tenses Made . . . Simple

The present tense describes an action that happens regularly. The past tense describes an action that has already taken place. The future tense describes an action that will take place in the future. Draw two lines under the predicate. Write the tense in the blank: **present**, **past**, or **future**.

_____ 1. **Jennifer returned her library books on time.**

_____ 2. **My parents will arrive at the dinner party by seven o'clock.**

_____ 3. **Our class recycles notebook paper and milk cartons.**

_____ 4. **Wai helps me with my fractions and decimals.**

_____ 5. **I watched *Myth Busters* with my dad and grandfather.**

_____ 6. **Alejandro will audition this Friday for the television show *Glee*.**

_____ 7. **Katie and I usually wear jeans every Saturday.**

_____ 8. **Maria called everyone on the donation list.**

Write a paragraph about any of your hobbies or activities (i.e., soccer, tennis, music lessons, etc.). Use at least three present tense predicates, two past tense predicates, and one future tense predicate. If necessary, use your dictionary.

_____

_____

_____

_____

_____

_____

_____

Scholastic Inc.   *Summer Express: Between Grades 5 & 6*

What Are the Chances?

Read each question below. Select the best answer using your knowledge of probability, statistics, odds, and ratios.

1. **Mark and Gil played a chip game using 15 chips. Four were red, three white, five green, and the rest were blue. What color will Gil most likely pick from the bag while not looking inside?**
   A. green
   B. blue
   C. red
   D. white

2. **If Mandy flips a quarter 100 times, how many times is she likely to have it land on heads?**
   A. 24
   B. 99
   C. 51
   D. 78

3. **Tony has a spinner that is equally divided into 6 sections. What is the probability he will land on 1 on his first spin?**
   A. $\frac{1}{3}$
   B. $\frac{1}{2}$
   C. $\frac{2}{3}$
   D. $\frac{1}{6}$

4. **Max rolled two identical dice together. What is the probability he will roll a 4 on either one?**
   A. $P = \left(\frac{1}{4}\right)$
   B. $P = \left(\frac{1}{6}\right)$
   C. $P = \left(\frac{1}{12}\right)$
   D. $P = \left(\frac{1}{3}\right)$

5. **Sam and Lee kept team stats for all 8 baseball games. The runs scored were as follows:**

Games:	#1	#2	#3	#4	#5	#6	#7	#8
Scores:	8	4	10	8	5	6	8	9

   What was the team's season average?
   A. 7.25
   B. 8.75
   C. 7.5
   D. 6.25

6. **Carson's math teacher had everyone select marbles from three boxes, each of which held 16 black and white marbles in different combinations. The drawings below illustrate the assignment and will help you as you complete the table to show the likelihood of Carson's outcomes based on rules of probability.**

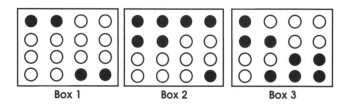

Box 1   Box 2   Box 3

Note: Each selection is tried only once by the students and all marbles are replaced for subsequent selections.

Selection #	Box #	Description	Probability
1	2	only white	
2	3	white or black	
3	1	black only	
4	1 & 3	white only	

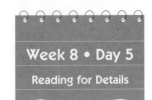

From Boy to President

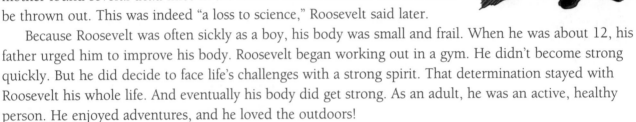

Do you know any 9-year-olds who have started their own museums? When Theodore Roosevelt was only 9, he and two of his cousins opened the "Roosevelt Museum of Natural History." The museum was in Theodore's bedroom. It had a total of 12 specimens. On display were a few seashells, some dead insects, and some birds' nests. Young Roosevelt took great pride in his small museum.

Born in New York in 1858, Theodore Roosevelt was not always healthy. "I was a sickly, delicate boy," he once wrote. Roosevelt had a health condition called asthma. He often found it hard to breathe. Instead of playing, he observed nature and then read and wrote about it.

Roosevelt's interest in nature sometimes got him into trouble. Once, his mother found several dead mice in the icebox. She demanded that the mice be thrown out. This was indeed "a loss to science," Roosevelt said later.

Because Roosevelt was often sickly as a boy, his body was small and frail. When he was about 12, his father urged him to improve his body. Roosevelt began working out in a gym. He didn't become strong quickly. But he did decide to face life's challenges with a strong spirit. That determination stayed with Roosevelt his whole life. And eventually his body did get strong. As an adult, he was an active, healthy person. He enjoyed adventures, and he loved the outdoors!

In 1900, at the age of 41, Roosevelt was elected Vice President. A year later, President McKinley was shot and killed. Roosevelt became our 26th President. At 42, he was the youngest leader the country had ever had.

Use the information you find in the passage to answer the following questions.

1. **What was the name of Teddy's museum?** _____

2. **How many specimens did the museum contain?** _____

3. **Name the three types of specimens.** _____

4. **What did Teddy Roosevelt's mother once find in her icebox?** _____

5. **What health condition did Teddy have as a boy?** _____

6. **What did Teddy's father encourage him to do?** _____

7. **In what year did Theodore Roosevelt become President?** _____

8. **Who was President when Theodore Roosevelt was Vice President?** _____

Scholastic Inc.   Summer Express: Between Grades 5 & 6

These are the skills your middle schooler will be working on this week.

Math
- Venn diagram
- logic
- geometry: irregular shapes
- problem solving

Reading
- reading for details

Writing
- summarizing
- writing an essay

Vocabulary
- word choice

Grammar
- editing for punctuation

Here are some activities you and your middle schooler might enjoy.

Then vs. Now Help your child find a board game he or she played as a little kid. It should be one that is familiar to your child and a fellow player. Your child should ask a friend or family member to play. Give your child the following instructions and challenges: First, see how fast you can play the game: roll the dice *fast*, move the piece *fast*, finish your turn *fast*, let the other player(s) play their turns *fast*, and so on. Second, try to make up new scenarios for the game based on the original rules of play, just embellished somewhat! It is always interesting to see things in a new way. Perhaps your child remembered the game as being very hard as a youngster, but now it is quite easy.

Lefty or Righty? You and your child should take up an unusual challenge: give your dominant hand a vacation! If you are a "lefty," brush your hair, brush your teeth, use a fork, etc., with the other (right) hand! If you're a "righty," use your left hand. Researchers say "hand preference" is biologically based and a function of the brain. It also is reported that activities such as this strengthen brain functions.

Your middle schooler might enjoy reading one of the following books:

Dragonwings
by Laurence Yep

*Steve Jobs and Steve Wozniack:
Geek Heroes Who Put the Personal in Computers*
by Mike Venezia

*A Little Princess: Being the Whole Story of
Sara Crewe Now Told for the First Time*
by Frances Hodgson Burnett

_____ 's Incentive Chart: Week 9

Name

This week, I plan to read_____ minutes each day.

CHART YOUR PROGRESS HERE.

Week 1	Day 1	Day 2	Day 3	Day 4	Day 5
I read for...	minutes	minutes	minutes	minutes	minutes
Put a sticker to show you completed each day's work.					

Congratulations!

Wow! You did a great job this week!

Place sticker here.

Parent or Caregiver's Signature_____

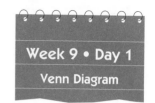
Data in a Venn Diagram

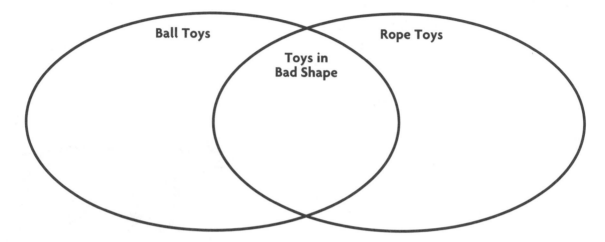

Ball Toys   Toys in
                 Bad Shape   Rope Toys

Maddie's Toy Story

My dog, Maddie, has acquired an affinity for tennis balls and rope toys. When I discovered this, I began to add these to her collection of toys. I spent time each night and on weekends with her playing catch or offering them as chew toys and fetch objects. Eventually, I began to notice her collection of balls and rope toys seemed to be growing rather ragged. So I set out to find and account for the items we had. Here are my findings. From her original treasure trove of 18 tennis balls and 11 rope toys, I found only 15 items. Of the six tennis balls I found, four were still in good shape; the rest were chewed beyond recognition. In the rope toy category, nine remained. Four of those nine rope toys were quite frayed at the ends, while the rest of that number would still do for more fun and games with Maddie.

Organize the story's information in the circle areas of the Venn Diagram based on toy's condition. In the overlap area, there will be a mix of rope toys and tennis balls that are badly chewed. Areas outside the diagram's lines may often be used to show they are similar, but do not fall into one of the categories of the Venn diagram.

1. **Of the 15 toys found, plot data on the diagram to show how each toy will be grouped.**

2. **How many are in the overlap?** _____ **List the types and number.**

_____

3. **How many balls are not represented on the diagram?** _____ **Explain your answer.**

_____

4. **What part of Maddie's 29 toys are not represented on the Venn diagram?** _____

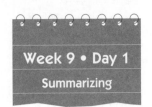

Summarizing Information

Read the following passage and then write a 20- to 30-word summary of the information on the lines provided. As you read, consider the "5Ws" and "1H" (*Who*?, *What*?, *When*?, *Where*?, *Why*?, and *How*?). This will help you when writing your summary.

A Dog's Life: From Wild Wolf to Friendly Fido

How does the family dog know from the look on your face that he or she is in the doghouse?

Believe it or not, your pooch did not learn from experience. There was no need. A recent study has found that dogs have an inborn talent for reading humans, an ability that may explain why they were one of people's first commonly kept pets.

A Survival Skill

Scientists have known for some time that dogs are the descendants of wolves. But they didn't know why some wolves could be domesticated, or tamed to live with, by humans.

Researcher Brian Hare says that he has a pretty good idea. He found that dogs are born with a remarkable ability to read people, making a human-dog relationship pretty natural.

Hare believes that wolves developed this people-reading skill as a way of survival. The wolves that became domesticated were the ones that could read humans well enough to find scraps of food. The better those wolves got at reading humans, the more food they found, which increased their chances of survival. Over thousands of years, those wolves turned into today's dogs.

Humans put dogs to good use, too. They used their new sidekicks to help them hunt, for protection, and for companionship.

Summary: _____

_____

_____

_____

_____

Scholastic Inc. Summer Express: Between Grades 5 & 6

Logically Speaking

What are the chances that you'll fly to Mars in your lifetime? No way, you say? But are you sure?

Describe the chances of each of the following events happening by choosing the best description from these choices: *certain, likely, unlikely, impossible.*

1. **There will be oxygen in the air tomorrow.** _____

2. **It will snow sometime next week.** _____

3. **Someone you know will be a senator one day.** _____

4. **Someone you know will live in another country one day.** _____

5. **A giraffe will walk down your block this year.** _____

6. **You'll have homework this week.** _____

7. **Your favorite performer will appear in your area.** _____

8. **You'll see an eclipse this month.** _____

9. **You will eat a strange food this week.** _____

10. **Scientists will discover something this year that will change your life.** _____

11. **Dolphins will someday be able to speak Chinese.** _____

12. **In your lifetime, you will work with a robot.** _____

Fascinating Women in History

So many women have had a great impact on history. They have explored unknown places and invented new creations. They have fought in the military and held political office. They have entertained us and made us think. They have changed the world. Begin by selecting a woman you would like to learn more about. Is there a woman who shared one of your hobbies or interests? Is there a woman whose actions you aspire to emulate? Any of the women listed at right would be an excellent subject to research. If you don't already have someone in mind, you can choose a name from the list.

Once you have a subject, you'll need an interesting title for your essay. A good title will introduce the reader to your topic and should grab the attention of your reader. When writing your essay, think about the audience who will be reading it. The more you can tell your audience about your subject, the more interesting your essay will be. What was your subject's childhood like? Did she have an issue about which she was passionate? What were some of the key events in your subject's life? Did her actions cause any changes? What was it that made your subject very successful or talented? The answers to any of these questions can make your paper interesting for your audience.

Famous Women

Susan B. Anthony
Marie Antoinette
Clara Barton
Shirley Temple Black
Pearl S. Buck
Marie Curie
Emily Dickinson
Amelia Earhart
Anne Frank
Indira Gandhi
Helen Keller
Billie Jean King
Maya Lin
Mother Theresa
Florence Nightingale
Rosa Parks
Queen Victoria
Eleanor Roosevelt
Sojourner Truth
Harriett Tubman
Oprah Winfrey

_____

_____

_____

_____

_____

_____

_____

_____

_____

Scholastic Inc.   Summer Express: Between Grades 5 & 6

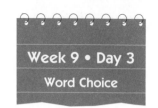

What Does It Mean?

Read the questions carefully. Circle the letter of the answer that is the best choice for the word meaning in that context. If necessary, use a dictionary or thesaurus.

1. **Which of the following remarks does not show reluctance?**
   A. "What's the rush?"
   B. "Let me think about it."
   C. "I want to leave now!"
   D. "Well, let's not be too hasty."

2. **In which of the following places would a pedestrian be?**
   A. Sitting on the sofa
   B. On the sidewalk
   C. Flying on an airplane
   D. Inside a city bus

3. **Which of the following would you personally not tolerate?**
   A. respect
   B. obedience
   C. an accident
   D. deceit

4. **Which of the following might not inspire you to persevere?**
   A. persistence
   B. idleness
   C. aspiration
   D. endurance

5. **Which of the following can be breached?**
   A. trick
   B. challenge
   C. agreement
   D. vacation

6. **Which one of the following would probably not cause a controversy?**
   A. closing a factory
   B. refusing to eat Brussels sprouts
   C. firing the mayor
   D. extending the school year

7. **Which of the following would not be a catastrophe?**
   A. earthquake
   B. hurricane
   C. a plane crash
   D. a picnic

8. **Which of the following can be quenched?**
   A. thirst
   B. diagram
   C. campfire
   D. ridicule

9. **Which of the following does not exclude even numbers?**
   A. 11, 13, 15, 17
   B. 2, 4, 6, 8, 10
   C. 1, 3, 5, 7, 9
   D. 13, 17, 19, 21

10. **Which of the following can be territorial?**
    A. dogwood
    B. treadmill
    C. tennis racket
    D. guard dog

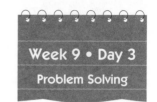
Mapmaker, Mapmaker

On a political map, regions that share borders often have different colors. Mathematicians have proved that no map needs more than four colors. Red, yellow, orange, blue—which four colors would you use to color a map of the world?

Color the maps using only the given number of colors.

1. **Use 3 colors.**

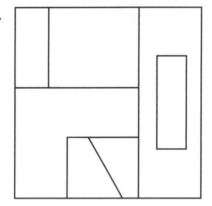

2. **Use 4 colors.**

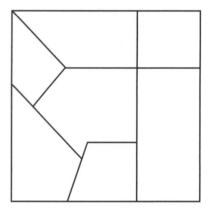

3. **Color this map using 4 colors.**

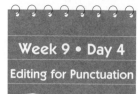

Find Mistakes—and Fix Them!

Carefully read the following sentences. Add punctuation—commas, semicolons, colons, periods, exclamation points, underlining, and quotation marks—where needed.

1. Laurie screamed Watch out

2. One is the name of my favorite song from the musical A Chorus Line

3. Leslie is the most talented pianist however she needs more practice.

4. Dr Mauldin announced I plan to treat her infections with antibiotics

5. On December 16 1773 colonists in Boston Massachusetts objected to British taxes

6. Jessica what can you tell the class about the Boston Tea Party asked Mr Starks.

7. Did the American Revolution begin on April 19 1775

8. When do we begin our cruise to the Greek Isles Turkey and Spain asked Marcus

9. Jennifer lives at 1517 Oak Grove Park Atlanta Georgia 30345

10. The Scott family traveled to the following islands Grenada Trinidad and Martinique

11. No Theresa Peter answered the call was not for you

12. Alex Kevin Jerry and Kenny stayed in the basement during the storm

13. The Caspian Sea the largest lake in the world has an area of 143550 square miles

14. Wow Mrs Porter actually offered Mark a job

15. Douglas asked Which route do we take to the Botanical Gardens

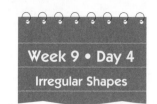

Area Irregulars

Estimate the area enclosed by each irregular shape's outline. To get a reasonable estimate:
1) Count all the squares that lie completely within the outline. **2)** Count all the squares through which the outline passes; these lie only partially within the outline. Divide this number by 2. **3)** Add the sum from steps 1 and 2.

1.

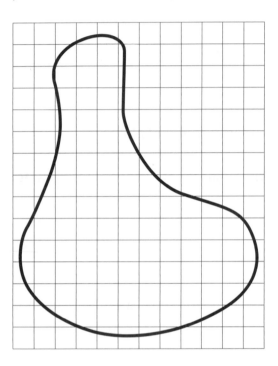

3.

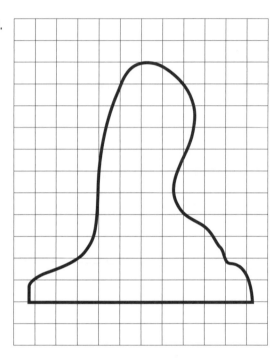

2.

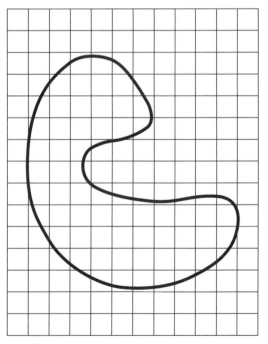

4.

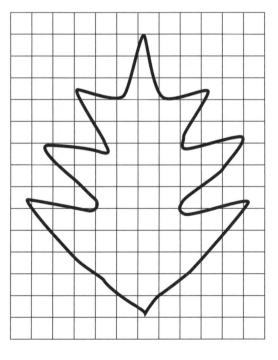

Scholastic Inc.   Summer Express: Between Grades 5 & 6

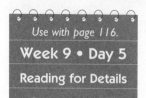
The Making of a Major Techie

William Henry Gates, III, was born October 28, 1955, in Seattle, Washington. He grew up in an upper-middle-class family with his older sister, Kristianne, and younger sister, Libby. Their father, William H. Gates, Jr., was a lawyer, and their mother, Mary Maxwell Gates, worked briefly as a teacher. She later gave up teaching to raise her children and work on civic affairs through various charities, including the United Way. She would often take Bill along on her volunteer work in schools and community organizations. Their relationship was a close one and only grew as a result of these shared times of volunteering and meeting people from varied backgrounds.

As a child, Bill showed a variety of interests. He relished playing board games, such as "Risk" and "Monopoly" and was often found reading reference books. His competitive side also came through during athletic games that he organized on summer vacations at the family's summer home on Puget Sound. At age 11 or 12, Bill's behavior in school began to worry his parents. He was doing well, but seemed bored and a bit withdrawn, so his parents enrolled him in Lakeside School at age 13. At Lakeside, Bill began to show enthusiasm for computers and computer programming. He did well in all of his subjects and excelled in math, science, drama, and English.

While at Lakeside School, a Seattle computer company offered to provide computer time for the students. A parents' association used proceeds from the school's rummage sale to purchase a Teletype terminal for students to use. Bill Gates became entranced with what a computer could do and spent much of his free time working at the terminal. He wrote a tic-tac-toe program in BASIC computer language that allowed users to play against the computer.

It was at Lakeside School where Bill met Paul Allen; the two became fast friends, bonding on their common enthusiasm over computers, even though their personalities were very different. Allen was more reserved and shy. Bill was feisty and at times combative. They both spent a great deal of their free time together working on programs. Occasionally, they would clash over who was right about a computer-related question or who should run the computer lab. On one occasion, Gates and Allen had their school computer privileges revoked for taking advantage of software glitches to get more free computer time from the company providing the computers. They were allowed back in the computer lab when they offered to debug the program. Bill later developed a payroll program for that same computer company.

Clearly Bill Gates was destined to develop a software company that spans the globe and attracts high respect from virtually all quarters.

Use the information you find in the passage to answer the following questions.

1. **What were the names of Bill Gates' sisters?**
   A. Lydia and Kristianne
   B. Libby and Kristianne
   C. Mary and Libby
   D. Sarah and Mary

2. **What board game(s) did Bill enjoy playing when he was younger?**
   A. Risk and Monopoly
   B. Chutes and Ladders
   C. Monopoly and Chess
   D. Dominoes and Risk

3. **How was Lakeside School important for Bill Gates?**
   A. His mother was on the board of the school.
   B. He and his wife Melinda formed a foundation to help the school.
   C. His parents enrolled him at Lakeside because it would be more challenging.
   D. His sisters attended the school and he could be with them.

4. **How would Bill's early relationship with Paul Allen be best described?**
   A. friendly, helpful, and silly
   B. cooperative, explosive, and professional
   C. estranged, awkward, and unhelpful
   D. casual, social, and distant

5. **Why was the computer lab at Lakeside important to Bill and Paul?**
   A. The computer lab gave them something to do other than play football.
   B. They had their parents buy the lab for the school.
   C. Bill and Paul broke all of the computers.
   D. They began writing computer programs.

6. **What was the name of a computer language Bill used?**
   A. Puget Sound
   B. English
   C. BASIC
   D. Teletype

7. **While he was at Lakeside, how did Bill help another company?**
   A. Bill created payroll and scheduling programs.
   B. Bill stopped hacking into the computer systems of the school and other businesses.
   C. He created games that the other students could play in their free time.
   D. He donated money to the school.

116

These are the skills your middle schooler will be working on this week.

Math
- word problems
- pictographs
- measuring angles
- area of a triangle

Reading
- reading for information: menus

Writing
- figurative language
- expository writing

Vocabulary
- math terms
- word choice

Grammar
- diagramming sentences

Here are some activities you and your middle schooler might enjoy.

Start a Collection Your child's collection could be pop tabs from drink cans, cut-outs or coupons from magazines and newspapers, or even delivery-food menus. Think of a creative and even odd use for these items. Chances are no one has a coupon-junk mail designed book cover or delivery-menu placemats. This collection exercises your brain.

What Is Your Opinion? Ask your middle schooler to "review" *this* book. What activities did he/she enjoy the most? What activities were the most helpful in preparing for the next grade?

Compound It Ask your child to list as many compound words as possible that contain the word *ball*. You may also want to try a variety of other words, such as *day*, *blue*, *hand*, or *water*.

Your middle schooler might enjoy reading one of the following books:

The Ruby in the Smoke
by Phillip Pullman

A Wrinkle in Time
by Madeleine L'Engle

The Case of the Case of Mistaken Identity
(The Brixton Brothers)
by Mac Barnett

's Incentive Chart: Week 10

_____
Name

This week, I plan to read_____ minutes each day.

CHART YOUR PROGRESS HERE.

Week 1	Day 1	Day 2	Day 3	Day 4	Day 5
I read for...	minutes	minutes	minutes	minutes	minutes
Put a sticker to show you completed each day's work.					

Congratulations!

Wow! You did a great job this week!

Place sticker here.

Parent or Caregiver's Signature_____

Dining at a Mexican Restaurant

Mayra's family is dining at a Mexican restaurant. Use the menu to answer the questions.

LA LINDA MEXICAN RESTAURANT
THE FRIENDLY TASTE OF MEXICO

APPETIZERS

Guacamole Dip	3.50
Cheese Dip	3.99
Bean Dip w/cheese	4.20
Queso Fandido	6.50
La Linda Wings	7.99

BURRITOS

Super Barrito	5.99
Burrito Ranchero	9.25
Burrito a La Linda	8.99
Seafood Burrito	8.50
Barrito Mexicano	7.99

FAJITAS

Presented steaming hot on a bed of peppers and onions. Served with rice, Mexi-beans, lettuce, pico de gallo, guacamole, sour cream, and flour tortillas.

Chicken	10.75
Steak	12.50
Shrimp	12.50
Baja Fajitas	13.50

ENCHILADAS

Super Enchiladas	7.50
Rancheras	7.50
Verdes	8.99
de Cerdo	8.25

QUESADILLAS

Cooked with pico de gallo and delightful Salsa Chipotle

Tilapia or Shrimp	9.55
Shredded Chicken	5.99
Ground Beef	5.99

SEAFOOD

Mango Salmon	13.50
Smothered Shrimp	11.50
Mexican Mahi-Mahi	13.99

CHIMICHANGA   7.99

Fried, rolled flour tortilla filled with seasoned, shredded chicken or beef, and Mexi-beans. Topped with cheese dip. Served with lettuce, tomatoes, guacamole and sour cream.

TACOS

Fish Tacos	9.99
Tacos de Brisket	9.99
Tacos de Asada	10.15
Tacos a la Brasa	10.15

STEAKS

Carne Asada	10.75
Steak Ranchero	10.75
Steak La Linda	14.50

Open for Lunch and Dinner Every Day
11:00 A.M. – 10:00 P.M.
22 Mill Road

1. **Where is the La Linda Mexican Restaurant located?**_____

2. **What is the least expensive appetizer Mayra's family can order? How much is it?**

_____

3. **What is the topping for the Chimichanga?** _____

4. **If Mayra orders Fajitas, what are the choices? How much is the least expensive type?**

_____

5. **Mayra's family ordered the following: 1 Cheese Dip; 1 Chimichanga; 1 Seafood Burrito; 1 Steak Fajita; and 1 Shrimp Quesadilla. What is their total check?**

_____

Scholastic Inc.   Summer Express: Between Grades 5 & 6

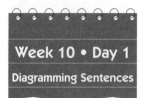

Sentence Maps: Direct Objects & Prepositional Phrases

Diagram the following sentences in the space provided. Study the example given. Use the correct form.

1. **Lauren read the book on vacation.**

   Lauren | read | book
   on vacation the

2. **During the storm, we lit candles.**

3. **Isabelle told the stories to the class.**

4. **Chris ate spaghetti and salad for dinner.**

5. **Marsh jumped into the pool.**

6. **Open the door.**

7. **Her plane arrived at 5:45 P.M. from Chicago.**

8. **The rabbit ran across the busy street.**

Scholastic Inc. *Summer Express: Between Grades 5 & 6*

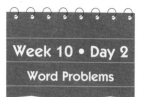

Word Problems—No Problem!

Solve the following word problems. If necessary, use a separate sheet of paper.

1. There were 4 factories that had to fill an order for 412 bicycles. How many bicycles does each factory need to make?

2. Gary purchased a used car. He paid $55 a month for 64 months. How much did he pay in all for the car?

3. Kenny has been collecting comic books since the age of 6. He collects about 40 books per year. If Kenny is now 12 years old, about how many comic books does he have?

4. Jane and Sam like to build kites. They're making a diamond kite that will be 20 inches long on each side. What will the kite's perimeter be?

5. Eliot is building a doghouse for his new puppy, Rocket. The doghouse will be $3\frac{1}{2}$ feet tall. How many inches high will it be?

6. The sum of these two numbers is 16. The product of these two numbers is 48. What are the two numbers?

7. Mr. Porter is installing a round swimming pool. The company says the pool will have a radius of 18 feet. What is the diameter?

8. Corey purchased a trail bike that cost $179.95. He was given a 20% discount. How much money did he save?

9. A major league baseball diamond is a square 90 feet long on each side. What is the perimeter? What is the area?

10. For charity, the track team jumped rope continuously for 10 hours. Taking turns, each member jumped at a pace of 55 times per minute. How many times did they jump rope during 10 hours?

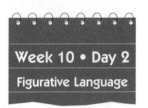

Figuratively Speaking!

Figurative language is language that means more than what it actually says on the surface. Figurative language can be used to add details to sentences, to add vividness and surprise, to clarify a point, or even to enhance your writing. The four kinds of figurative language are **metaphors**, **similes**, **hyperbole**, *and* **personification**. *The two most common figures of speech are similes and metaphors.*

- *A simile makes a comparison between two unlike things, using* like *or* as.
  Example: She was quiet as a mouse.

- *A metaphor makes a comparison between two unlike things, without using* like *or* as.
  Example: The road was a ribbon of moonlight.

- *A personification gives human characteristics and qualities to nonhuman things, like animals.*
  Example: The moon peeked through the clouds and smiled down on us.

- *A hyperbole is an exaggerated statement used to heighten the effect.*
  Example: The ice-cream sundae had toppings that were a mile high.

Select the best answer for the following questions.

1. **Which of the following is not a figure of speech?**
   A. metaphor
   B. simile
   C. alliteration
   D. hyperbole

2. **"The old mansion frowned down at us from the top of the hill" is an example of a**
   A. metaphor.
   B. personification.
   C. simile.
   D. hyperbole.

3. **"She was out like a light" is an example of**
   A. simile.
   B. hyperbole.
   C. metaphor.
   D. personification.

4. **Figurative language adds which of the following things to your writing?**
   A. vividness
   B. surprise
   C. obstacle
   D. A and B

5. **"The sea licked the grass at the edge of the shore." This sentence is an example of a**
   A. metaphor.
   B. personification.
   C. simile.
   D. hyperbole.

6. **Jonathan's feet were houseboats! This sentence is an example of a**
   A. metaphor.
   B. personification.
   C. hyperbole.
   D. simile.

Using Pictographs

The following pictographs contain data from the Eagle Woods Middle School's Happy-Gram sales for 2009 and 2010. Use the information shown to answer the questions.

2009 Happy-Gram Sales Data
☺ = 24 Happy-Grams

Homeroom	Students Participating	Happy-Grams Sold
Mr. Casey	30	☺☺☺☺☺
Mr. Davis	28	☺☺☺☺☺
Mrs. Ng	29	☺☺☺☺☺
Mrs. Gold	30	☺☺☺
Mrs. Harper	27	☺☺
Mrs. Evors	29	☺☺☺☺

2010 Happy-Gram Sales Data
☺ = 24 Happy-Grams

Homeroom	Students Participating	Happy-Grams Sold
Mr. Casey	20	☺☺☺☺
Mr. Davis	30	☺☺☺
Mrs. Ng	30	☺☺☺
Mrs. Gold	28	☺☺☺☺☺
Mrs. Harper	29	☺☺☺☺☺☺
Mrs. Evors	25	☺☺☺

1. **The sales in 2009 for Mrs. Evors' homeroom exceeded which class or classes that year?**
   A. Mrs. Harper's and Mr. Davis's
   B. Mrs. Ng's, Mrs. Harper's, and Mr. Casey's
   C. Mrs. Gold's and Mrs. Harper's
   D. only Mrs. Gold's

2. **All of Mr. Casey's participants sold the same amount in 2009. How many did each participant sell?**
   A. 6
   B. 4
   C. 60
   D. 120

3. **What is the total sales amount for Mr. Davis' class in 2009 & 2010?**
   A. 72
   B. 168
   C. 250
   D. 192

4. **Which class sold a total of 240 in both years combined?**
   A. Mr. Casey's
   B. Mrs. Harper's
   C. Mr. Davis's
   D. Mrs. Evors'

Inform Your Reader About . . .

Expository writing *is a type of writing, the purpose of which is to inform, explain, describe, or define the author's subject to the reader. Expository text is meant to deposit information. Examples of this type of writing are cooking instructions, driving directions, and instructions on performing a task. Key words such as* first, after, next, then, *and* last *usually signal sequential writing. The creator of an expository text cannot assume that the reader or listener has prior knowledge or prior understanding of the topic being discussed. One important point to keep in mind is to try to use words that clearly show what you are talking about rather than blatantly telling the reader what is being discussed.*

Write an expository paragraph on one of the following topics. Be sure to state your problem and list one or more solutions for the problem. **Remember:** Your task is to inform, explain, describe, or define.

1. **Is your school community doing its part to help take care of the environment? Write a paragraph describing how "green" your school really is.**

2. **Are there problems with our modern day Olympics? Describe things that don't work well and how they might be improved.**

3. **Can you brainstorm a list of issues that you would like our president to address? What course of action should he take?**

4. **You have learned this year what it takes to be a fifth grader, what teachers expect of you, and how to succeed as a student. Write a letter that gives fifth grade students specific advice on what they really need to know before they enter sixth grade.**

_____

_____

_____

_____

_____

_____

Scholastic Inc. Summer Express: Between Grades 5 & 6

What's Your Angle?

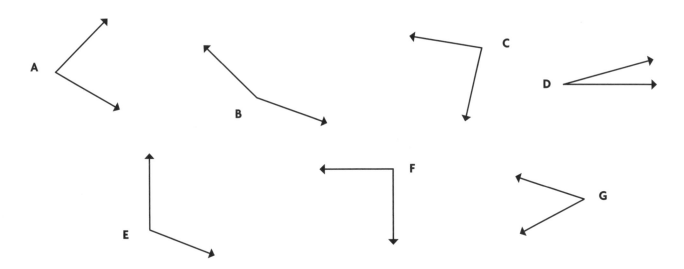

Study the angles above and answer the questions below using what you know about angles. Some questions require the use of a protractor.

1. **Which angle is a right angle?** _____

2. **What is the measure of a right angle?** _____

3. **List the obtuse angles:** _____

4. **List the acute angles:** _____

5. **What is the measurement of angle D?** _____

6. **What is the measurement of angle B?** _____

7. **How much smaller is angle D than angle A?** _____

8. **What would angle A measure if it were increased by 15°?** _____

9. **What would angle E measure if it were decreased 5°?** _____

10. **Draw a 70° angle.**

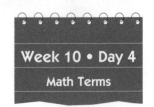

Word Search

Find each of the words in the Word Bank in the puzzle.

```
D E V Q B N R M P H P H H O V D V O K M N P B
A N E V G H W A U A W M G J N F I K L K C H D
N J G C E F N A G L S G L E O J T A A Q M M V
D I A Q M T S A E J T B D S C X X C M G S J V
S P T E L P J P O S K I S M N F M S F E P U I
H T G V E K S M B U V E P C N W J F Q L T M W
R H V L R N R Q X I R A P L P I F W O G Y E G
T R A P E Z O I D D R S L A E M I Z P I G Y R
K Y O E N G M U R A P Q Y Z H T G J T Y J E A
X N U M E R A T O R F U L O I K F W C O N S L
R O T C A F R V H H A S F S F A X C Z C V C T
F I V M B N G C C M W G C O K E C Y G V Z R F
V T N F U I N T E G E R A O S Q P U U S I R U
L A I K F D A U X O I T A R S U B E B A A R I
I M T B Z R T N M S N L J P D O J A N C I D A
C I R C U M F E R E N C E Z E T L G T D A D N
L T G O Z H T J C P R O B A B I L I T Y E D W
J S A B W R H R E C T A N G L E O I Z Y S E O
I E X B Y H E M C S Z L L E W N N C T X N Z L
A Y Y E J P Z U W S W P A S Q T C B K L E S G
```

Scholastic Inc.   Summer Express: Between Grades 5 & 6

WORD BANK

CHORD	GEOMETRY	RADIUS
CIRCUMFERENCE	INTEGER	RATIO
DIAMETER	MULTIPLE	RECTANGLE
DIVIDEND	NUMERATOR	ROMAN NUMERALS
ESTIMATION	PERCENT	TANGRAM
FACTOR	PROBABILITY	TRAPEZOID
FRACTION	QUOTIENT	TRIANGLE

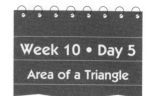
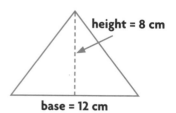

Triangles

The formula for finding the area of a triangle: is $A = \frac{1}{2} \times b \times h$

Example: $A = \frac{1}{2} \times (12 \times 8)$

$A = \frac{1}{2} \times 96$

$A = 48$ sq cm

height = 8 cm

base = 12 cm

Label the triangles with the information given and solve to find the area.

1. Figure 1 is an acute triangle with a base measurement of 7.5 cm and its height is 12 cm. Find the area of this triangle.

figure 1

2. Figure 2 is an acute triangle with a base measurement of 14 cm and its height is 9 cm. Find the area of this triangle.

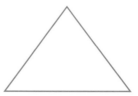

figure 2

3. Figure 3 is a right triangle. The base is 2 cm long and the height is 10 cm. Find the area of this triangle.

figure 3

4. Figure 4 is an obtuse triangle. The base is 12 cm long and the height is 1.5 cm. Find the area of this triangle.

figure 4

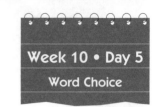

Boost Your Vocabulary

Make your writing more powerful by boosting your vocabulary. Read the list of interesting words below. Choose four words you'd like to learn and look them up in a dictionary. On the lines provided, identify the part of speech (noun, verb, adjective, adverb), write a definition in your own words, then use the word in a sentence.

alabaster	blarney	passe	noisome	thespian
maven	appease	queue	coerce	gaffe
cuisine	pandemic	intrigue	envoy	potpourri
relinquish	rustic	bustle	cosmopolitan	etiquette
odious	vermilion	acronym	ambience	absolve

1. _____ _____ _____
   (word)   (part of speech)   (definition)

   _____

   _____

2. _____ _____ _____
   (word)   (part of speech)   (definition)

   _____

   _____

3. _____ _____ _____
   (word)   (part of speech)   (definition)

   _____

   _____

4. _____ _____ _____
   (word)   (part of speech)   (definition)

   _____

   _____

Scholastic Inc.   Summer Express: Between Grades 5 & 6

Answer Key

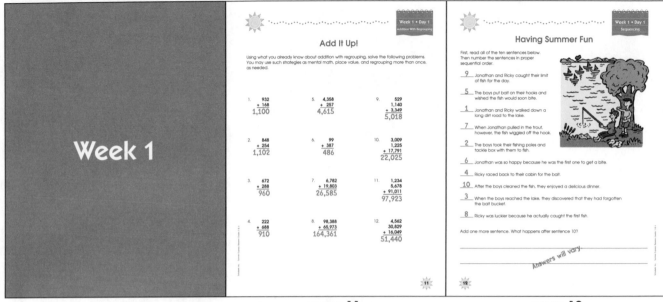

Week 1

page 11

Add It Up!

Using what you already know about addition with regrouping, solve the following problems. You may use such strategies as mental math, place value, and regrouping more than once, as needed.

1.	932 + 168 **1,100**	5.	4,358 + 257 **4,615**	9.	529 1,140 + 3,349 **5,018**
2.	848 + 254 **1,102**	6.	99 + 387 **486**	10.	3,009 1,225 + 17,791 **22,025**
3.	672 + 288 **960**	7.	6,782 + 19,803 **26,585**	11.	1,234 5,678 + 91,011 **97,923**
4.	222 + 688 **910**	8.	98,388 + 65,973 **164,361**	12.	4,562 30,829 + 16,049 **51,440**

11

page 12

Having Summer Fun

First, read all of the ten sentences below. Then number the sentences in proper sequential order.

9 Jonathan and Ricky caught their limit of fish for the day.

5 The boys put bait on their hooks and wished the fish would soon bite.

1 Jonathan and Ricky walked down a long dirt road to the lake.

7 When Jonathan pulled in the trout, however, the fish wiggled off the hook.

2 The boys took their fishing poles and tackle box with them to fish.

6 Jonathan was so happy because he was the first one to get a bite.

4 Ricky raced back to their cabin for the bait.

10 After the boys cleaned the fish, they enjoyed a delicious dinner.

3 When the boys reached the lake, they discovered that they had forgotten the bait bucket.

8 Ricky was luckier because he actually caught the first fish.

Add one more sentence. What happens after sentence 10?

_____

_____ *Answers will vary.*

12

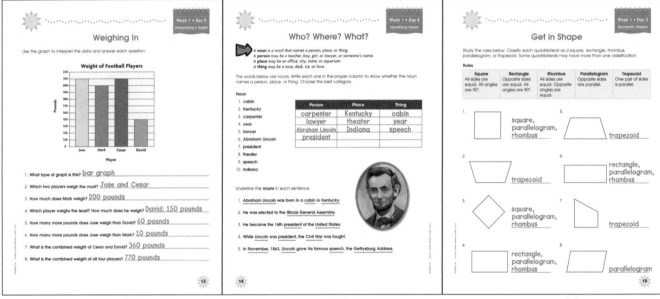

page 13

Weighing In

Use the graph to interpret the data and answer each question.

Weight of Football Players

(bar graph with Pounds on y-axis, Player on x-axis: Jose, Mark, Cesar, David)

1. What type of graph is this? **bar graph**
2. Which two players weigh the most? **Jose and Cesar**
3. How much does Mark weigh? **200 pounds**
4. Which player weighs the least? How much does he weigh? **David; 150 pounds**
5. How many more pounds does Jose weigh than David? **60 pounds**
6. How many more pounds does Jose weigh than Mark? **10 pounds**
7. What is the combined weight of Cesar and David? **360 pounds**
8. What is the combined weight of all four players? **770 pounds**

13

page 14

Who? Where? What?

A **noun** is a word that names a person, place, or thing.
A **person** may be a teacher, boy, girl, or lawyer, or someone's name.
A **place** may be an office, city, state, or aquarium.
A **thing** may be a nose, desk, ice, or love.

The words below are nouns. Write each one in the proper column to show whether the noun names a person, place, or thing. Choose the best category.

Noun

1. cabin
2. Kentucky
3. carpenter
4. year
5. lawyer
6. Abraham Lincoln
7. president
8. theater
9. speech
10. Indiana

Person	Place	Thing
carpenter	Kentucky	cabin
lawyer	theater	year
Abraham Lincoln	Indiana	speech
president		

Underline the **nouns** in each sentence.

1. Abraham Lincoln was born in a cabin in Kentucky.
2. He was elected to the Illinois General Assembly.
3. He became the 16th president of the United States.
4. While Lincoln was president, the Civil War was fought.
5. In November, 1863, Lincoln gave his famous speech, the Gettysburg Address.

14

page 15

Get in Shape

Study the rules below. Classify each quadrilateral as a square, rectangle, rhombus, parallelogram, or trapezoid. Some quadrilaterals may have more than one classification.

Rules

Square	Rectangle	Rhombus	Parallelogram	Trapezoid
All sides are equal. All angles are 90°.	Opposite sides are equal. All angles are 90°.	All sides are equal. Opposite angles are equal.	Opposite sides are parallel.	One pair of sides is parallel.

1. **square, parallelogram, rhombus**
5. **trapezoid**

2. **trapezoid**
6. **rectangle, parallelogram, rhombus**

3. **square, parallelogram, rhombus**
7. **trapezoid**

4. **rectangle, parallelogram, rhombus**
8. **parallelogram**

15

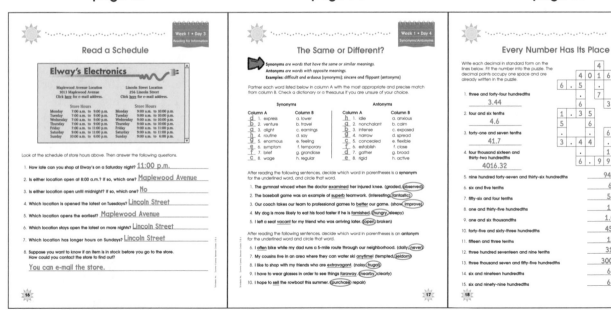

page 16

Read a Schedule

Elway's Electronics

Maplewood Avenue Location	Lincoln Street Location
1013 Maplewood Avenue	256 Lincoln Street
Click here for e-mail address.	Click here for e-mail address.

Store Hours (Maplewood Avenue)
Monday 7:00 a.m. to 9:00 p.m.
Tuesday 7:00 a.m. to 9:00 p.m.
Wednesday 7:00 a.m. to 9:00 p.m.
Thursday 7:00 a.m. to 9:00 p.m.
Friday 7:00 a.m. to 11:00 p.m.
Saturday 9:00 a.m. to 11:00 p.m.
Sunday 10:00 a.m. to 6:00 p.m.

Store Hours (Lincoln Street)
Monday 9:00 a.m. to 10:00 p.m.
Tuesday 9:00 a.m. to 10:00 p.m.
Wednesday 9:00 a.m. to 10:00 p.m.
Thursday 9:00 a.m. to 10:00 p.m.
Friday 9:00 a.m. to 11:00 p.m.
Saturday 9:00 a.m. to 11:00 p.m.
Sunday 9:00 a.m. to 6:00 p.m.

Look at the schedule of store hours above. Then answer the following questions.

1. How late can you shop at Elway's on a Saturday night? **11:00 p.m.**
2. Is either location open at 8:00 a.m.? If so, which one? **Maplewood Avenue**
3. Is either location open until midnight? If so, which one? **No**
4. Which location is opened the latest on Tuesdays? **Lincoln Street**
5. Which location opens the earliest? **Maplewood Avenue**
6. Which location stays open the latest on more nights? **Lincoln Street**
7. Which location has longer hours on Sundays? **Lincoln Street**
8. Suppose you want to know if an item is in stock before you go to the store. How could you contact the store to find out?
   You can e-mail the store.

16

page 17

The Same or Different?

Synonyms are words that have the same or similar meanings.
Antonyms are words with opposite meanings.
Examples: difficult and arduous (synonyms); sincere and flippant (antonyms)

Partner each word listed below in column A with the most appropriate and precise match from column B. Check a dictionary or a thesaurus if you are unsure of your choice.

Synonyms

Column A	Column B
d 1. express	a. lower
b 2. venture	b. travel
a 3. alight	c. earnings
h 4. routine	d. say
g 5. enormous	e. feeling
c 6. symptom	f. temporary
f 7. brief	g. grandiose
e 8. wage	h. regular

Antonyms

Column A	Column B
h 1. idle	a. anxious
c 2. nonchalant	b. calm
a 3. intense	c. exposed
g 4. narrow	d. spread
f 5. concealed	e. flexible
b 6. establish	f. close
d 7. gather	g. broad
e 8. rigid	h. active

After reading the following sentences, decide which word in parentheses is a **synonym** for the underlined word, and circle that word.

1. The gymnast winced when the doctor examined her injured knee. (graded, (observed))
2. The baseball game was an example of superb teamwork. (interesting, (fantastic))
3. Our coach takes our team to professional games to better our game. (show, (improve))
4. My dog is more likely to eat his food faster if he is famished. ((hungry), sleepy)
5. I left a seat vacant for my friend who was arriving later. ((open), broken)

After reading the following sentences, decide which word in parentheses is an **antonym** for the underlined word and circle that word.

6. I often bike while my dad runs a 5-mile route through our neighborhood. (daily, (never))
7. My cousins live in an area where they can water ski anytime! (tempted, (seldom))
8. I like to shop with my friends who are extravagant. (noisy, (frugal))
9. I have to wear glasses in order to see things faraway. ((nearby), clearly)
10. I hope to sell the rowboat this summer. ((purchase), repair)

17

page 18

Every Number Has Its Place

Write each decimal in standard form on the lines below. Fit the number into the puzzle. The decimal points occupy one space and are already written in the puzzle.

1. three and forty-four hundredths **3.44**
2. four and six tenths **4.6**
3. forty-one and seven tenths **41.7**
4. four thousand sixteen and thirty-two hundredths **4016.32**
5. nine hundred forty-seven and thirty-six hundredths **947.36**
6. six and five tenths **6.5**
7. fifty-six and four tenths **56.4**
8. one and thirty-five hundredths **1.35**
9. one and six thousandths **1.006**
10. forty-five and sixty-three hundredths **45.63**
11. fifteen and three tenths **15.3**
12. three hundred seventeen and nine tenths **317.9**
13. three thousand seven and fifty-five hundredths **3007.55**
14. six and nineteen hundredths **6.19**
15. six and ninety-nine hundredths **6.99**

18

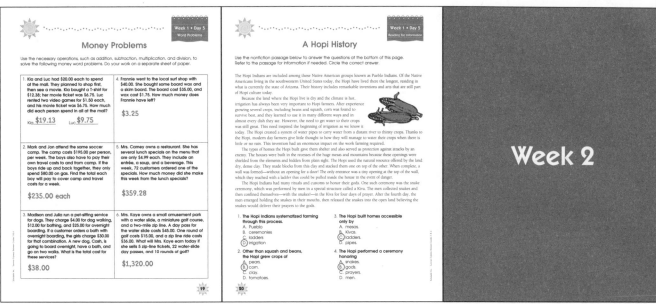

Week 1 • Day 5
Word Problems

Money Problems

Use the necessary operations, such as addition, subtraction, multiplication, and division, to solve the following money word problems. Do your work on a separate sheet of paper.

1. Kia and Luc had $20.00 each to spend at the mall. They planned to shop first, then see a movie. Kia bought a T-shirt for $12.38; her movie ticket was $6.75. Luc rented two video games for $1.50 each, and his movie ticket was $6.75. How much did each person spend in all at the mall?
   Kia $19.13 Luc $9.75

2. Mark and Jon attend the same soccer camp. The camp costs $195.00 per person, per week. The boys also have to pay their own travel costs to and from camp. If the boys ride up and back together, they only spend $80.00 on gas. Find the total each boy will pay to cover camp and travel costs for a week.
   $235.00 each

3. Madison and Julia run a pet-sitting service for dogs. They charge $4.00 for dog walking, $12.00 for bathing, and $25.00 for overnight boarding. If a customer orders a bath with overnight boarding, the girls charge $30.00 for that combination. A new dog, Cash, is going to board overnight, have a bath, and go on two walks. What is the total cost for these services?
   $38.00

4. Frannie went to the local surf shop with $40.00. She bought some board wax and a skim board. The board cost $35.00, and wax cost $1.75. How much money does Frannie have left?
   $3.25

5. Mrs. Carney owns a restaurant. She has several lunch specials on the menu that are only $4.99 each. They include an entrée, a soup, and a beverage. This week, 72 customers ordered one of the specials. How much money did she make this week from the lunch specials?
   $359.28

6. Mrs. Kaye owns a small amusement park with a water slide, a miniature golf course, and a two-mile zip line. A day pass for the water slide costs $45.00. One round of golf costs $15.00, and a zip line ride costs $36.00. What will Mrs. Kaye earn today if she sells 5 zip-line tickets, 22 water-slide day passes, and 10 rounds of golf?
   $1,320.00

page 19

Week 1 • Day 5
Reading for Information

A Hopi History

Use the nonfiction passage below to answer the questions at the bottom of this page. Refer to the passage for information if needed. Circle the correct answer.

The Hopi Indians are included among those Native American groups known as Pueblo Indians. Of the Native Americans living in the southwestern United States today, the Hopi have lived there the longest, residing in what is currently the state of Arizona. Their history includes remarkable inventions and arts that are still part of Hopi culture today.

Because the land where the Hopi live is dry and the climate is hot, irrigation has always been very important to Hopi farmers. After experience growing several crops, including beans and squash, corn was found to survive best, and they learned to use it in many different ways and in almost every dish they ate. However, the need to get water to their crops was still great. This need inspired the beginning of irrigation as we know it today. The Hopi created a system of water pipes to carry water from a distant river to thirsty crops. Thanks to the Hopi, modern day farmers give little thought to how they will manage to water their crops when there is little or no rain. This invention had an enormous impact on the work farming required.

The types of homes the Hopi built gave them shelter and also served as protection against attacks by an enemy. The houses were built in the recesses of the huge mesas and mountains because these openings were shielded from the elements and hidden from plain sight. The Hopi used the natural resource offered by the land: dry, dense clay. They made blocks from this clay and stacked them one on top of the other. When complete, a wall was formed—without an opening for a door! The only entrance was a tiny opening at the top of the wall, which they reached with a ladder that could be pulled inside the house in the event of danger.

The Hopi Indians had many rituals and customs to honor their gods. One such ceremony was the snake ceremony, which was performed by men in a special structure called a Kiva. The men collected snakes and then confined themselves—with the snakes!—in the Kiva for four days of prayer. After the fourth day, the men emerged holding the snakes in their mouths, then released the snakes into the open land believing the snakes would deliver their prayers to the gods.

1. **The Hopi Indians systematized farming through this process.**
   A. Pueblo
   B. ceremonies
   C. ladders
   (D.) irrigation

2. **Other than squash and beans, the Hopi grew crops of**
   A. pears.
   (B.) corn.
   C. clay.
   D. tomatoes.

3. **The Hopi built homes accessible only by**
   A. mesas.
   B. Kivas.
   (C.) ladders.
   D. pipes.

4. **The Hopi performed a ceremony honoring**
   A. snakes.
   (B.) gods.
   C. prayers.
   D. men.

page 20

Week 2

Week 2 • Day 1
Suffixes

Building Vocabulary

*A **suffix** is a word part that is added to the **end** of a word and changes its part of speech and its meaning. For example, adding the suffix –er to read (a verb) makes the new word reader (a noun). Adding –less to face (a noun) makes faceless (an adjective).*

Suffix	Meaning	Example	Meaning
-er	one who	bak**er**	one who bakes
	that which	dic**er**	device that chops or dices
-or	one who	debt**or**	one who owes a debt
-able/-ible	can be made/done, having the quality of	wash**able**	can be washed
		valu**able**	having value
		deduct**ible**	can be deducted
		sens**ible**	having sense

Write the word that is formed by adding the given suffix to each of the following words. Write a basic meaning of the new word. **Remember:** Check the spelling of the new word. Sometimes a letter is added and other times a letter might be omitted. If necessary, use a dictionary.

Example: win + -*er* winner one who wins

1. **like + -*able*** likable can be liked
2. **advise + -*or*** advisor one who advises
3. **resist + -*ible*** resistible can be resisted
4. **bat + -*er*** batter one who bats
5. **depend + -*able*** dependable can be relied on
6. **write + -*er*** writer one who writes

page 23

Week 2 • Day 1
Job Interview

Camp Counselor Job Interview

Ms. Starks, the camp leader, received your application for Junior Camp Counselor. She has called you in for an interview. The interview will be a chance for the camp leader to ask you questions. The questions might be about your family, friends, interests, possible future plans, as well as your job skills. To prepare for the interview, write out answers to the questions. Then ask one of your family members to interview you as if he or she is Ms. Starks. Your interviewer can also come up with additional questions. **Remember:** Answer using complete sentences.

* **What is your age and school grade?** ______________________
* **How many people are in your family?** ______________________
* **Where do you live? How long have you lived there?** ______________________
* **What are some of your favorite hobbies?** ______________________
* **What is your favorite sport?** ______________________
* **What is your favorite game that is not an electronic game or video game?** ______________________
* **Why do you think you are qualified for this job?** ______________________
* **Have you ever had a job before? Tell me about that.** ______________________
* **What are your plans for the future?** ______________________
* **What would you like to be or do when you are an adult?** ______________________

Answers will vary.

page 24

Week 2 • Day 2
Simplifying Fractions

Geographic Wonders

What is the world's largest country? The largest desert? The smallest continent? Do this fraction match-up to discover the answers. Each geographic "wonder" listed below is followed by a fraction. Reduce the fraction to its lowest terms. Then correctly match it to one of the fractions in the right column and you'll find the name of the geographic wonder or its location. Write that name or place on the line.

Geographic Wonders			Place	
1. **World's largest desert**	$\frac{39}{312}$	Sahara	$\frac{1}{7}$	Australia
2. **Largest country (land)**	$\frac{2}{18}$	Russia	$\frac{1}{5}$	China
3. **World's largest city**	$\frac{19}{38}$	Tokyo	$\frac{1}{4}$	Canada
4. **Highest waterfall**	$\frac{100}{110}$	Salto Angel	$\frac{1}{8}$	Sahara
5. **Largest country (population)**	$\frac{6}{30}$	China	$\frac{2}{3}$	Mammoth – Flint Ridge
6. **Smallest continent**	$\frac{3}{21}$	Australia	$\frac{10}{11}$	Salto Angel in Venezuela
7. **Largest cave system**	$\frac{12}{18}$	Mammoth	$\frac{1}{6}$	Nile
8. **World's highest mountain**	$\frac{3}{9}$	Everest	$\frac{1}{3}$	Everest
9. **Second largest country**	$\frac{12}{48}$	Canada	$\frac{1}{9}$	Russia
10. **World's longest river**	$\frac{5}{30}$	Nile	$\frac{1}{2}$	Tokyo, Japan

page 25

Week 2 • Day 2
Sequencing

Jumbled Sentences

Rewrite the following words and phrases in the correct order to create a complete sentence.

1. wall is on the in the kitchen. The clock
   The clock is on the wall in the kitchen.
2. for the city bus. Zachary is waiting
   Zachary is waiting for the city bus.
3. Katie piano. is playing the grand
   Katie is playing the grand piano.
4. living room. in the There are mirrors not any
   There are not any mirrors in the living room.
5. my bed. on The dog is sleeping shaggy
   The shaggy dog is sleeping on my bed.
6. opening the front door. Aunt Margie is not
   Aunt Margie is not opening the front door.
7. are Lei and Shane looking the right place. in
   Lei and Shane are looking in the right place.
8. Jennifer the chapter of is writing novel. last her
   Jennifer is writing the last chapter of her novel.

page 26

Week 2 • Day 3
Parts of Speech

The Family Dinner

Do not read the story yet! Give it to a partner and ask him or her to tell you the part of speech under each blank below. You say a word for the part of speech, and your partner writes it in the blank. Then he or she writes the words where they belong in the story and reads the story aloud. Now you have created a hilarious story!

1. ________ NOUN
2. ________ (-ING) VERB
3. ________ ADVERB
4. ________ PLURAL NOUN
5. ________ VERB
6. ________ PAST-TENSE VERB
7. ________ PLURAL NOUN
8. ________ PLURAL NOUN
9. ________ ADJECTIVE
10. ________ ADVERB

Lei's family is Chinese-American. Once a week, they serve a traditional Chinese dinner. This week Lei invited her friend Carla, to have ________ (1) with them.

Lei's mother was very busy ________ (2) dinner when Carla arrived. ________ (3) Carla sensed all of the smells coming from the kitchen. Lei's mother asked the girls to set the table. The ________ (4) gave each person a pair of chopsticks, a soup bowl, a soup spoon, and a rice bowl.

Carla asked, "Where are the knives and forks?"

Lei replied, "You won't need those. We always use chopsticks! I'll show you how to ________ (5) them."

Then the girls ________ (6) into the kitchen where Lei's father was chopping vegetables. Suddenly, he threw all the ________ (7) into a large cooking pan that was coated with very hot cooking oil. Lei remarked, "That's a wok!"

Lei's mother started pouring various ________ (8) onto large platters. Lei asked Carla, "Will you help me take the platters to the table?" Carla carried the bowl of rice to the table. There were so many ________ (9) dishes, such as stir-fried beef, steamed vegetables, sweet and sour chicken, and wontons.

Carla wanted to use the chopsticks but failed miserably. She tried picking up a piece of beef, but it ________ (10) flew across the table landing in Lei's father's plate. Everyone laughed but continued eating the delicious food. Then Lei showed Carla how to use the chopsticks.

Answers will vary.

page 27

Week 2 • Day 3
Subject-Verb Agreement

Making Subjects and Verbs Agree

*A verb must agree with its subject in number. Number refers to whether a word is **singular** (naming one) or **plural** (naming more than one). A noun that is singular must have a singular form of the verb. A noun that is plural takes the plural form of a verb.*

Examples:

Cynthia enjoys cooking for her friends and relatives. (singular subject and singular verb)
Many cats sleep during the day. (plural subject and plural verb)

In each sentence, circle the subject. Then underline the verb in the parentheses that agrees with the subject.

1. The first (TV system) (was demonstrated, were demonstrated) at the New York World's Fair in 1939.
2. Early television (sets) (was, were) large black and white models.
3. Today, though, technical (advancements) (gives, give) us very high-quality color pictures.
4. (Television) (brings, bring) the world into our living rooms with pictures and sounds.
5. Almost all (televisions) (comes, come) with stereo or surround sound.
6. Until the 1960s, each (city) (was given, were given) only four or five TV channels.
7. Now, (cable TV) (brings, bring) hundreds of channels to our televisions.
8. A (TV producer) usually (decides, decide) which stories to cover in the newscast.
9. News (photographers) (carries, carry) video cameras to record, or film, the stories they cover.
10. A news (item) usually (lasts, last) between 20 and 90 seconds.

page 28

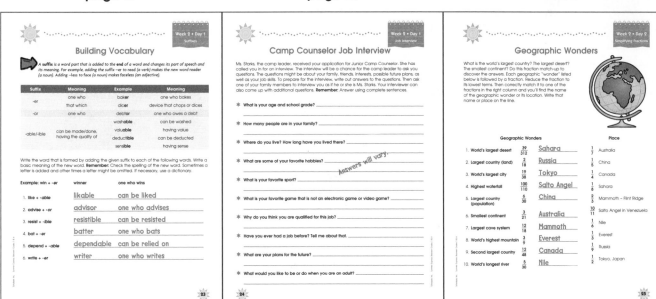

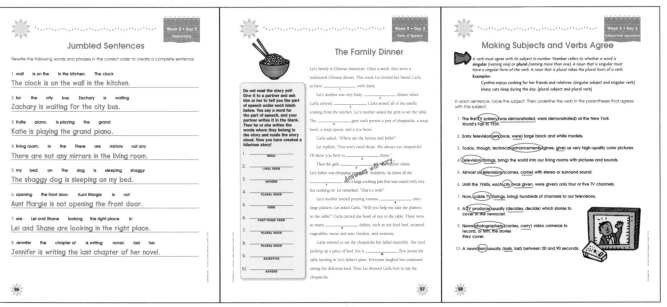

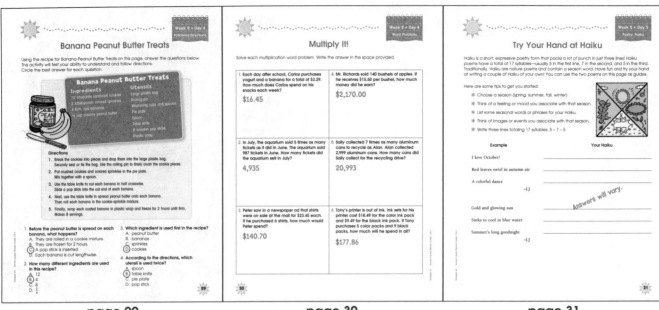

page 29

Banana Peanut Butter Treats

Using the recipe for Banana Peanut Butter Treats on this page, answer the questions below. This activity will test your ability to understand and follow directions. Circle the best answer for each question.

Banana Peanut Butter Treats

Ingredients
- 12 chocolate sandwich cookies
- 2 tablespoons colored sprinkles
- 4 firm, ripe bananas
- ¼ cup creamy peanut butter

Utensils
- Large plastic bag
- Rolling pin
- Measuring cups and spoons
- Pie plate
- Spoon
- Table knife
- 8 wooden pop sticks
- Plastic wrap

Directions
1. Break the cookies into pieces and drop them into the large plastic bag. Securely seal or tie the bag. Use the rolling pin to finely crush the cookie pieces.
2. Put crushed cookies and colored sprinkles in the pie plate. Mix together with a spoon.
3. Use the table knife to cut each banana in half crosswise. Slide a pop stick into the cut end of each banana half.
4. Next, use the table knife to spread peanut butter onto each banana. Then roll each banana in the cookie-sprinkle mixture.
5. Finally, wrap each coated banana in plastic wrap and freeze for 2 hours until firm. Makes 8 servings.

1. Before the peanut butter is spread on each banana, what happens?
A. They are rolled in a cookie mixture.
B. They are frozen for 2 hours.
C. A pop stick is inserted.
D. Each banana is cut lengthwise.

2. How many different ingredients are used in this recipe?
A. 12
B. 4
C. 8
D. 2

3. Which ingredient is used first in the recipe?
A. peanut butter
B. bananas
C. sprinkles
D. cookies

4. According to the directions, which utensil is used twice?
A. spoon
B. table knife
C. pie plate
D. pop stick

---

page 30

Multiply It!

Solve each multiplication word problem. Write the answer in the space provided.

1. Each day after school, Carlos purchases yogurt and a banana for a total of $3.29. How much does Carlos spend on his snacks each week?
$16.45

2. In July, the aquarium sold 5 times as many tickets as it did in June. The aquarium sold 987 tickets in June. How many tickets did the aquarium sell in July?
4,935

3. Peter saw in a newspaper ad that shirts were on sale at the mall for $23.45 each. If he purchased 6 shirts, how much would Peter spend?
$140.70

4. Mr. Richards sold 140 bushels of apples. If he receives $15.50 per bushel, how much money did he earn?
$2,170.00

5. Sally collected 7 times as many aluminum cans to recycle as Alan. Alan collected 2,999 aluminum cans. How many cans did Sally collect for the recycling drive?
20,993

6. Tony's printer is out of ink. Ink sets for his printer cost $18.49 for the color ink pack and $9.49 for the black ink pack. If Tony purchases 5 color packs and 9 black packs, how much will he spend in all?
$177.86

---

page 31

Try Your Hand at Haiku

Haiku is a short, expressive poetry form that packs a lot of punch in just three lines! Haiku poems have a total of 17 syllables—usually 5 in the first line, 7 in the second, and 5 in the third. Traditionally, Haiku are nature poems and contain a season word. Have fun and try your hand at writing a couple of Haiku of your own! You can use the two poems on this page as guides.

Here are some tips to get you started:
- Choose a season (spring, summer, fall, winter).
- Think of a feeling or mood you associate with that season.
- List some seasonal words or phrases for your Haiku.
- Think of images or events you associate with that season.
- Write three lines totaling 17 syllables: 5 - 7 - 5

Example

I love October!
Red leaves swirl in autumn air
A colorful dance
—LJ

Gold and glowing sun
Sinks to cool in blue water
Summer's long goodnight
—LJ

Your Haiku

Answers will vary.

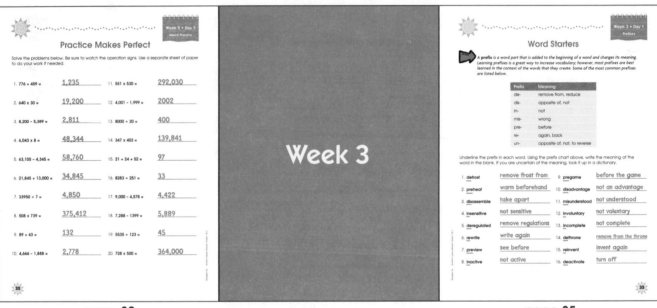

page 32

Practice Makes Perfect

Solve the problems below. Be sure to watch the operation signs. Use a separate sheet of paper to do your work if needed.

1. 776 + 459 = **1,235**
2. 640 x 30 = **19,200**
3. 8,200 - 5,389 = **2,811**
4. 6,043 x 8 = **48,344**
5. 63,105 - 4,345 = **58,760**
6. 21,845 + 13,000 = **34,845**
7. 33950 ÷ 7 = **4,850**
8. 508 x 739 = **375,412**
9. 89 + 43 = **132**
10. 4,666 - 1,888 = **2,778**
11. 551 x 530 = **292,030**
12. 4,001 - 1,999 = **2002**
13. 8000 ÷ 20 = **400**
14. 347 x 403 = **139,841**
15. 21 + 24 + 52 = **97**
16. 8283 ÷ 251 = **33**
17. 9,000 - 4,578 = **4,422**
18. 7,288 - 1399 = **5,889**
19. 5535 ÷ 123 = **45**
20. 728 x 500 = **364,000**

Week 3

---

page 35

Word Starters

A **prefix** is a word part that is added to the beginning of a word and changes its meaning. Learning prefixes is a great way to increase vocabulary; however, most prefixes are best learned in the context of the words that they create. Some of the most common prefixes are listed below.

Prefix	Meaning
de-	remove from, reduce
dis-	opposite of, not
in-	not
mis-	wrong
pre-	before
re-	again, back
un-	opposite of, not, to reverse

Underline the prefix in each word. Using the prefix chart above, write the meaning of the word in the blank. If you are uncertain of the meaning, look it up in a dictionary.

1. defrost — **remove frost from**
2. preheat — **warm beforehand**
3. disassemble — **take apart**
4. insensitive — **not sensitive**
5. deregulated — **remove regulations**
6. rewrite — **write again**
7. preview — **see before**
8. inactive — **not active**
9. pregame — **before the game**
10. disadvantage — **not an advantage**
11. misunderstood — **not understood**
12. involuntary — **not voluntary**
13. incomplete — **not complete**
14. dethrone — **remove from the throne**
15. reinvent — **invent again**
16. deactivate — **turn off**

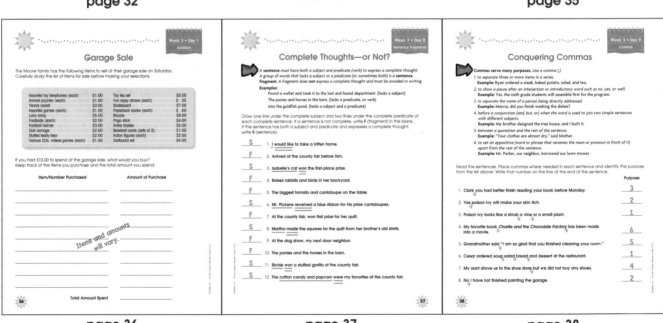

page 36

Garage Sale

The Moore family has the following items to sell at their garage sale on Saturday. Carefully study the list of items for sale before making your selections.

Assorted toy telephones (each)	$1.00	Toy tea set	$5.00
Animal puzzles (each)	$1.00	Fun sippy straws (each)	$.25
Tennis racket	$3.00	Skateboard	$7.00
Assorted games (each)	$1.00	Paperback books (each)	$.50
Lava lamp	$5.00	Bicycle	$8.00
Footballs (each)	$2.50	Pogo stick	$4.00
Football helmet	$3.00	Roller blades	$5.00
Doll garage	$2.50	Baseball cards (sets of 3)	$1.50
Stuffed teddy bear	$2.00	Action figures (each)	$2.00
Various CDs, videos games (each)	$1.00	Dartboard set	$4.00

If you had $10.00 to spend at the garage sale, what would you buy? Keep track of the items you purchase and the total amount you spend.

Item/Number Purchased	Amount of Purchase

Items and amounts will vary.

Total Amount Spent

---

page 37

Complete Thoughts—or Not?

A **sentence** must have both a subject and predicate (verb) to express a complete thought. A group of words that lacks a subject or a predicate (or sometimes both) is a **sentence fragment**. A fragment does not express a complete thought and must be avoided in writing.
Examples:
Found a wallet and took it to the lost and found department. (lacks a subject)
The ponies and horses in the barn. (lacks a predicate, or verb)
Into the goldfish pond. (lacks a subject and a predicate)

Draw one line under the complete subject and two lines under the complete predicate of each complete sentence. If a sentence is not complete, write **F** (fragment) in the blank. If the sentence has both a subject and predicate and expresses a complete thought, write **S** (sentence).

S 1. I would like to take a kitten home.
F 2. Arrived at the county fair before him.
S 3. Isabelle's cat won the first-place prize.
F 4. Raises rabbits and birds in her backyard.
F 5. The biggest tomato and cantaloupe on the table.
S 6. Mr. Pickens received a blue ribbon for his prize cantaloupes.
F 7. At the county fair, won first prize for her quilt.
S 8. Martha made the squares for the quilt from her brother's old shirts.
F 9. At the dog show, my next door neighbor.
F 10. The ponies and the horses in the barn.
S 11. Richie won a stuffed gorilla at the county fair.
S 12. The cotton candy and popcorn were my favorites at the county fair.

---

page 38

Conquering Commas

Commas serve many purposes. Use a comma (,)
1. to separate three or more items in a series.
   Example: Ryan ordered a steak, baked potato, salad, and tea.
2. to show a pause after an interjection or introductory word such as no, yes, or well.
   Example: Yes, the sixth grade students will assemble first for the program.
3. to separate the name of a person being directly addressed.
   Example: Marcia, did you finish washing the dishes?
4. before a conjunction (and, but, or) when the word is used to join two simple sentences with different subjects.
   Example: My brother designed the tree house, and I built it.
5. between a quotation and the rest of the sentence.
   Example: "Your clothes are almost dry," said Mother.
6. to set an appositive (word or phrase that renames the noun or pronoun in front of it) apart from the rest of the sentence.
   Example: Mr. Parker, our neighbor, borrowed our lawn mower.

Read the sentences. Place commas where needed in each sentence and identify the purpose from the list above. Write that number on the line at the end of the sentence.

	Purpose
1. Clark, you had better finish reading your book before Monday.	3
2. Yes, poison ivy will make your skin itch.	2
3. Poison ivy looks like a shrub, a vine, or a small plant.	1
4. My favorite book, *Charlie and the Chocolate Factory*, has been made into a movie.	6
5. Grandmother said, "I am so glad that you finished cleaning your room."	5
6. Cesar ordered soup, salad, bread, and dessert at the restaurant.	1
7. My aunt drove us to the shoe store, but we did not buy any shoes.	4
8. No, I have not finished painting the garage.	2

page 39

Fraction Subtraction

Find each difference. Reduce. Study the example below.

Example:

$6\frac{2}{3} = \frac{20}{3} \times \frac{4}{4} = \frac{80}{12}$

$-3\frac{1}{4} = \frac{13}{4} \times \frac{3}{3} = \frac{39}{12}$

$\frac{41}{12} = 3\frac{5}{12}$

1. Change any mixed numbers to improper fractions.
2. Find the least common denominator and rewrite fraction.
3. Subtract. Reduce if necessary.

1. $8\frac{3}{4}$
   $-4\frac{2}{3}$
   $4\frac{1}{12}$

4. $16\frac{5}{8}$
   $-4\frac{3}{4}$
   $11\frac{7}{8}$

7. $6\frac{1}{2}$
   $-5\frac{1}{3}$
   $1\frac{1}{6}$

2. $10\frac{1}{3}$
   $-2\frac{2}{5}$
   $7\frac{14}{15}$

5. $8\frac{1}{2}$
   $-3\frac{2}{7}$
   $5\frac{3}{14}$

8. $14\frac{5}{8}$
   $-5\frac{3}{4}$
   $8\frac{5}{8}$

3. $9\frac{4}{5}$
   $-7\frac{6}{10}$
   $2\frac{1}{5}$

6. $8\frac{9}{10}$
   $-3\frac{2}{5}$
   $5\frac{1}{2}$

9. $11\frac{2}{3}$
   $-1\frac{1}{4}$
   $9\frac{1}{4}$

page 40

Fixing Run-On Sentences

*A **run-on sentence** is a sentence with at least two independent clauses (complete sentences or thoughts) that are forced together instead of being properly connected or separated.*
To correct run-on sentences, there are several options:
1. Separate clauses using punctuation.
2. Separate clauses using a conjunction.
3. Rearrange the sentence (by adding or removing words).
Example: Lauren smeared sunscreen on her arms and face, the sun was extremely hot.
Corrected form: Lauren smeared sunscreen on her arms and face because the sun was extremely hot.
Example: Walker received a new puppy for his birthday he named the puppy Rover.
Corrected form: Walker received a new puppy for his birthday. He named it Rover.

Correct the following run-on sentences by using any of the above options.

1. Melinda likes reading mystery novels it sometimes makes her sleepy.
   Melinda likes reading mystery novels, but it sometimes makes her sleepy.

2. When I am older I want to have a big family, I really like big families.
   I really like big families and want to have one when I'm older.

3. Christine looked out the window she saw that it was raining.
   Christine looked out the window and saw that it was raining.

4. Our family usually leaves for the park at 10:30 today we are going at 10:00 instead.
   Our family usually leaves for the park at 10:30, but today we're going at 10:00 instead.

5. To make this project you will need 15 index cards you will also need several colored markers
   To make this project, you will need 15 index cards and several colored markers.

page 41

Fighting for Their Lives

Amazon Basin, Brazil – The Yanomami Indians in northern Brazil think it is the end of the world. And for the remaining 9,000 tribe members, it could be. Recently, fires raging in the rain forests endangered the Yanomami's homes, food supply, and health. But the fires are not the only threat to the Yanomami and other tribal people living in the Amazon rain forest.

Lumber companies are cutting down trees. Mining companies are digging up the land for gold. Gold was discovered on the Yanomami reserve in the 1980s. About 20,000 miners descended on the area. The miners brought diseases that killed many of the native people.

The Yanomami live in the secluded rain forests along the Brazil-Venezuela border. Their culture is very old; it dates back 3,000 years. The life of the tribe has not changed much in all that time. Some Yanomami had no direct contact with the outside world until last decade.

The Juma people also live in the Amazon rain forests. Less than 100 years ago, there were thousands of Juma living in the forests. Now only six Juma remain. The Juma still eat traditional foods and hunt with bows and arrows. Since they have contact with the outside world, it is common for them to wear modern clothing. Recently, the last young Juma warrior was killed by a jaguar.

"The Yanomami are heading for where the Juma are now," says Pam Kraft, who educates the public about native people. There are 250 million indigenous, or native, people who belong to endangered tribes around the world. The basic human rights of these people are recognized, but their rights to their land, their resources, and their culture are not.

Firefighters from all over the world flew to Brazil in response to the fire threatening the homes of the Yanomami. In the jungle, the tribal people held ceremonies, praying for rain to come and quench the fire. The rains came and began to extinguish the flames. The threat of the fire is over, but the Yanomami still face many urgent problems. They are still in danger.

"The future of these people is related to our behavior," says Sydney Posseulo, of the Federal Indian Bureau in Brazil. "We have to show more support for their way of life."

page 42

Circle the letter with the best answer for each question.

1. Why have the Yanomami remained mostly unchanged for 3,000 years?
   A. They've had no reason to leave their lands.
   B. They live without outside influences.
   C. They weren't allowed to leave the forests.
   D. They didn't know about modern tools and conveniences.

2. How did the discovery of gold cause the deaths of many Yanomami?
   A. They caught diseases from the miners.
   B. The miners killed the Yanomami to get the gold.
   C. The Yanomami moved off their land.
   D. The Yanomami died of starvation.

3. What does "The Yanomami are heading for where the Juma are now" mean?
   A. The Yanomami will live near the Juma.
   B. The Yanomami tribe will soon be as close to extinction as the Juma tribe is now.
   C. The Yanomami tribe is going the wrong way.
   D. The Yanomami and Juma travel together.

4. How were the fires in the rain forests finally extinguished?
   A. Firefighters flew to Brazil.
   B. Tribal people prayed.
   C. People held ceremonies.
   D. The rains came.

Circle the letter with the best definition of the underlined word.

5. Many people don't recognize the tribes' rights to the <u>resources</u> of their land.
   A. things available to use
   B. traditional clothing
   C. culture
   D. music

6. Firefighters from all over the world flew to Brazil in <u>response</u> to the fire.
   A. refusal
   B. fear
   C. quiet manner
   D. reaction or reply

7. Mining companies arrived when they heard there was gold in the rain forest.
   A. having to do with fires
   B. having to do with extinction
   C. having to do with digging for minerals or metals
   D. having to do with rain forests

8. The rains came and began to <u>extinguish</u> the flames.
   A. spread
   B. put out
   C. increase
   D. avoid

page 43

Create a Superhero

Create your own superhero! Describe your superhero's powers or strengths. However, give your superhero one weakness. Describe the weakness and how he or she would keep it a secret or overcome it. On a separate sheet of paper, sketch your superhero in action!

Answers will vary.

page 44

What's in a Name?

The tables below show every letter of the alphabet partnered with a numeric value. Use this "code" to determine how much your name would be worth by spelling your name and jotting down the value for each letter in it. Then add those numbers to get your total "name value." Try calculating the name values of your friends and family, too.

A	B	C	D	E	F	G	H	I	J	K	L	M
765	134	55	700	32	19	76	400	94	40	148	1,000	363

N	O	P	Q	R	S	T	U	V	W	X	Y	Z
2,500	157	601	822	344	999	650	975	238	89	12	36	4

Write your name on this line and use the white space to do your computations.

1. _____

Use the chart and numbers to find the values of the names of friends and family members.

2. _____ = _____
   (Friend's Name)   *Answers will vary.*

3. _____ = _____
   (Family Member's Name)

Week 4

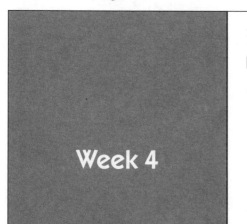

page 47

At Home With Homophones

Homophones are words that have the same pronunciation, but different spellings and different meanings.
Example: My little brother (ate/eight) all (ate/eight) pieces of candy.

Underline the correct homophone in the following sentences.

1. We need to take a (break, brake) from this strenuous work.

2. The sales clerk wanted to (cell, sell) as many (sell, cell) phones as possible.

3. Ross wants his socks because his (tows, toes) are freezing.

4. Jason is going to (wear, ware) his work boots to work today.

5. The new (principal, principle) asked for a meeting of all the parents.

6. Mother does not want to talk about the (passed, past) events in her life.

7. May I go to the birthday party, (to, too, two)?

8. During the math test, the teacher walked down the (aisle, isle) to the back of the room.

9. Zachary has one favorite (pare, pair, pear) of jeans.

10. (Who's, Whose) brown cell phone is that on the corner of the desk?

page 48

Plotting Coordinates on a Graph

Plot each of the given ordered pairs on the coordinate plane below. Note: Ordered pairs or "coordinates" are written with respect to the **x** axis & **y** axis (x, y). See example given.

Amy's Rainfall Record—2011

Rainfall in Inches / Month of the Year

1. (1, 0) ✓
2. (3, 4)
3. (6, 7)
4. (8,2)
5. (2,1)
6. (4,12)
7. (5,10)
8. (9,3)
9. (12,1)
10. (7, 2)
11. (10, 5)
12. (11, 6)

Week 4 • Day 2
Researching Information

Where in the World?

Where in the world would you find the following cities and geographical features? Research any locations you are not familiar with. Write the country name on the blank.

1. Rome, Naples, Mount Vesuvius — Italy
2. Nile River, Cairo, Suez Canal — Egypt
3. Madrid, Barcelona, Iberian Mountains — Spain
4. Sydney, Great Victoria Desert, Melbourne — Australia
5. Mount Fuji, Hiroshima, Osaka — Japan
6. Cape Town, Johannesburg, Drakensberg Mountains — South Africa
7. Paris, Marseille, Alps — France
8. Toronto, Rocky Mountains, Victoria Island — Canada
9. Hamburg, Black Forest, Danube River — Germany
10. Casablanca, Atlas Mountains, Rabat — Morocco
11. Acapulco, Rio Grande, Baja California — Mexico
12. New Delhi, Ganges River, Deccan Plateau — India
13. Mount Katahdin, Chicago, San Diego — United States
14. São Paolo, Amazon Basin, Rio de Janeiro — Brazil

page 49

Week 4 • Day 2
Proofreading Symbols

Using Proofreading Symbols

There are 21 errors in this passage. Read the excerpt. As you find the mistakes, make the appropriate marks to indicate each of the errors. If a change, insertion, or omission is needed, make those changes as well.

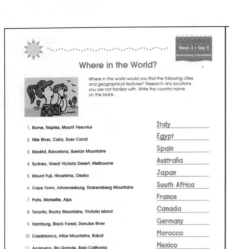

Symbol	Explanation
≡	Capitalize a letter
/	Lowercase a letter
⊙	Add a period
^	Add a comma
ℓ	Delete a word or a punctuation mark
^	Insert a word or a punctuation mark
sp	Correct spelling
¶	Begin a new paragraph

Yoga Partners

Meg, and her mom had been going to a wednesday night yoga class togather for about a year Several of Megs friends and their Moms even choze to join them. It was fun relaxing, and challenging. Meg really loved being with her mom as well as taking care of her own body. Meg's mom Alex was a Nurse and had always encouraged her and, her brother to eat well and to particpate in activities they liked. So far, yoga was Meg's favorite but she still played on her school's tennis team and swam every summer on her her neighborhood swim team.

Every Wednesday about 4:30 Meg and her mom ate a light dinner of soup and her mom's famous cheese-veggie wrap's. their class began at 6:00 and lasted one our. Meg loved the way Yoga made her feel because it stretched and toned her muscles. Most of all, Meg and her mom enjoed the deep breathing and meditative quality that caused them to focus on the present moment

page 50

Week 4 • Day 3
Multiplication

Multiplication Mastery

Find the products for the following multiplication problems.

1. 976 x 719 = 701,744
2. 328 x 446 = 146,288
3. 899 x 719 = 646,381
4. 950 x 568 = 539,600
5. 493 x 587 = 289,391
6. 755 x 582 = 439,410
7. 763 x 167 = 127,421
8. 665 x 469 = 311,885
9. 800 x 983 = 786,400
10. 974 x 314 = 305,836
11. 681 x 737 = 501,897
12. 175 x 465 = 81,375
13. 903 x 941 = 849,723
14. 670 x 262 = 175,540
15. 536 x 329 = 176,344
16. 688 x 640 = 440,320

page 51

Week 4 • Day 3
Context Clues

Giants of the Earth

Think of your favorite tree. Is it big? Next to a **towering** sequoia, it would probably look tiny.

Sequoias are very special trees. They are some of the largest and oldest living things on Earth.

Once, there were many different kinds of sequoias. Now, there are only two kinds left. These are the coastal redwoods and the big trees. The **coastal** redwoods grow near the Pacific Ocean. The coastal redwoods are the tallest trees on Earth. Many are over 300 feet tall. That is as tall as a 30-story building! The area where these trees grow is **nicknamed** "the Land of the Giants."

The big trees, or giant sequoias, do not grow along the coast. They are **located** farther inland, in California. The big trees are much wider and heavier than the coastal redwoods. Think of a giraffe and an elephant. This will give you an idea of the difference between the two kinds of sequoias. The coastal redwoods are the "giraffes." The big trees are the "elephants."

The biggest sequoia of all is a big tree called General Sherman. It is one of the most **massive** living things on Earth. This tree is 275 feet tall. It is not as tall as some of the redwoods, but its trunk is the widest. It is more than 100 feet around. Scientists think it weighs more than 6,000 tons!

Sequoias take a long time to get so big. Humans grow for about 20 years, then they stay the same height. Sequoias keep growing as long as they live, and that can be a long time! Scientists say that General Sherman is between 3,000 and 4,000 years old. Think of everything that tree has seen in its lifetime!

Find each vocabulary word in the selection. The words and sentences around it will help you figure out its meaning. Circle the letter with the best definition of the underlined word.

1. **Next to a towering redwood, most trees look tiny.**
   A. made of metal
   B. angry
   C. very tall (circled)
   D. very heavy
2. **The coastal redwoods grow near the Pacific Ocean.**
   A. like a roller coaster
   B. mysterious
   C. to slide down a hill
   D. along the coast (circled)
3. **The area where the coastal redwoods grow is nicknamed "the land of the Giants."**
   A. given a name that describes a special feature (circled)
   B. figured out a tree's height
   C. decided how much a tree weighs
   D. cut down
4. **The big trees are located inland.**
   A. growing
   B. found in a place (circled)
   C. stored
   D. at the shore
5. **The big tree called General Sherman is one of the most massive living things on Earth.**
   A. bossy
   B. enormous (circled)
   C. full of lumps
   D. interesting

page 52

Week 4 • Day 4
Summarizing Information

Whales in a Noisy Ocean

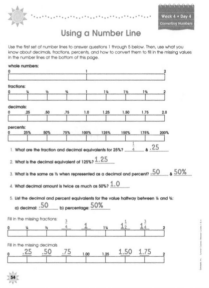

Read the article below. Then identify journalism's "5 Ws and 1 H" (Who? What? When? Where? Why? How?) to complete the table with the corresponding information from the article. (There may be more than one answer.) Finally, use your notes to write a 20-word summary.

Washington – Whales use sound in very different ways. Some whales produce songs that travel over vast distances. They also use echolocation, like bats, to locate food and find their way. But other noise in the ocean creates a problem for the whales.

Since 1987, the International Fund for Animal Welfare (IFAW) has sent their research vessel *Song of the Whale* around the world to provide a platform for marine research and education. During the travels, the *Song of the Whale* scientists have developed expertise in using underwater microphones to listen to and record the sounds that the animals make. This helps them to track, identify, and survey different species.

One of the threats facing whales and other marine animals is noise pollution in the seas, such as noise from drilling, military activities, oil exploration, and coastal construction. This noise can cause great distress to whales and dolphins and can result in injury and even death.

It is feared this noise pollution may cause mass strandings, when large numbers come ashore and beach together. If the *Song of the Whale* team can track the whales and identify their habitats, then hopefully the nature and location of disturbing noise can be changed.

Who?	
What?	
When?	Answers will vary.
Where?	
Why?	
How?	

Write a 20-word summary.

page 53

Week 4 • Day 4
Converting Numbers

Using a Number Line

Use the first set of number lines to answer questions 1 through 5 below. Then, use what you know about decimals, fractions, percents, and how to convert them to fill in the missing values in the number lines at the bottom of this page.

whole numbers: 0, 1, 2

fractions: 0, ¼, ½, ¾, 1, 1¼, 1½, 1¾, 2

decimals: 0, .25, .50, .75, 1.0, 1.25, 1.50, 1.75, 2.0

percents: 0, 25%, 50%, 75%, 100%, 125%, 150%, 175%, 200%

1. What are the fraction and decimal equivalents for 25%? $\frac{1}{4}$ & .25
2. What is the decimal equivalent of 125%? 1.25
3. What is the same as ½ when represented as a decimal and percent? .50 & 50%
4. What decimal amount is twice as much as 50%? 1.0
5. List the decimal and percent equivalents for the value halfway between ¼ and ¾:
   a) decimal: .50 b) percentage: 50%

Fill in the missing fractions: 0, ¼, ½, $\frac{3}{4}$, 1, 1¼, $1\frac{1}{2}$, $1\frac{3}{4}$, 2

Fill in the missing decimals: 0, .25, .50, .75, 1.00, 1.25, 1.50, 1.75, 2

page 54

Use with page 56.
Week 4 • Day 5
Reading for Information

The Arctic: Closer Than You Think

The next time you get caught in a rainstorm, you might have the icy Arctic to thank. It may sound strange, but it's true. This region at the top of the world affects us all. And we affect it!

The Arctic may seem like a foreign land. But scientists say Arctic weather has an impact on weather all over the world. This is how: Cold, dry air forms over the Arctic, and then wind currents shift this cold air to the south. When this cold air hits warm, wet air, storms form. These storms are part of weather patterns that travel around the globe.

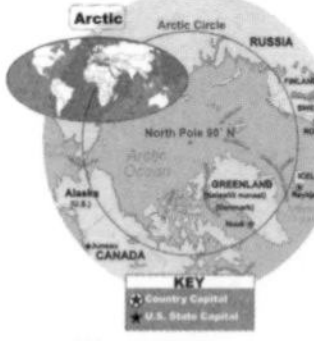

The circle drawn shows the Arctic region.

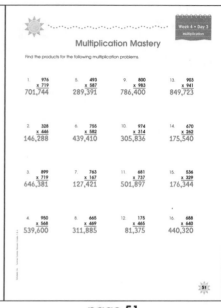

An Unwanted Gift

The Arctic might bring rainstorms to our part of the world. But what we bring to the Arctic can be much worse. Wind and water carry chemicals from factories in the United States and other countries to the Arctic. There the frigid Arctic environment functions like a freezer. Chemicals last for a long time in the atmosphere around the North Pole. These chemicals get into the food supply. The animals and people of the Arctic region can get sick from drinking polluted water. They can get ill from eating polluted food.

Science at the North Pole

Because so much pollution ends up in the Arctic, scientists say it's a good place to study the environment. They examine the icy ocean. They study the nearby land. They test the Arctic air. That gives them an idea of how much pollution the world is creating. It tells them about the health of the whole planet.

page 55

Use with page 55.
Week 4 • Day 5
Reading for Information

Answer the following questions based on the information you read in the passage. Circle the letter of the correct response.

1. **The center of the Arctic region is at**
   A. the North Pole (circled)
   B. the South Pole
   C. Greenland
   D. Alaska
2. **Look at the map. Which of these is not part of the Arctic region?**
   A. Asia
   B. North America
   C. Africa (circled)
   D. Europe
3. **Arctic weather affects weather all over the world because**
   A. It is extremely cold.
   B. Arctic winds move south and form storm patterns that travel around the globe. (circled)
   C. Arctic air is polluted.
   D. Chemicals last a long time near the North Pole.
4. **Why is the Arctic a good place for scientists to study air and water pollution?**
   A. The Arctic has clean air and water.
   B. Pollution from all over the world collects in the Arctic. (circled)
   C. No one bothers the scientists there.
   D. The Arctic Ocean is at the North Pole.
5. **The amount of pollution in the Arctic tells scientists**
   A. How much pollution the world is creating. (circled)
   B. That it is too polluted for people to live there.
   C. That people should stop working in factories.
   D. That chemicals will get into the food supply.
6. **Animals and people in the Arctic region can get sick from**
   A. Living in freezing temperatures.
   B. Drinking polluted water. (circled)
   C. Experiencing stormy weather patterns.
   D. Testing the air and water.
7. **Why might the Arctic seem like a foreign land?**
   A. It's a great place to go on vacation.
   B. Many people live there.
   C. Scientists study it.
   D. It's very different from where we live. (circled)
8. **Look at the map. Which of these cities is a state capital?**
   A. Juneau (circled)
   B. Nuuk
   C. Reykjavik
   D. Oslo

page 56

Week 5

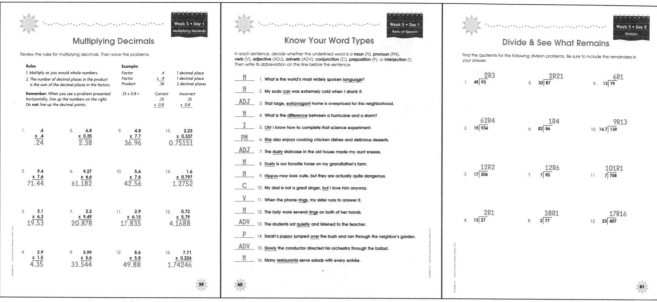

Week 5 • Day 1
Multiplying Decimals

Multiplying Decimals

Review the rules for multiplying decimals. Then solve the problems.

Rules

1. Multiply as you would whole numbers.
2. The number of decimal places in the product is the sum of the decimal places in the factors.

Example:

Factor	*.4*	*1 decimal place*
Factor	*x .9*	*1 decimal place*
Product	*.36*	*2 decimal places*

Remember: *When you see a problem presented horizontally, line up the numbers on the right. Do* **not** *line up the decimal points.*

.35 x 0.8 = Correct: *.35 x 0.8* Incorrect: *.35 x 0.8*

1. .6 x .4 = .24
5. 6.8 x 0.35 = 2.38
9. 4.8 x 7.7 = 36.96
13. 2.23 x 0.337 = 0.75151
2. 9.4 x 7.6 = 71.44
6. 9.27 x 6.6 = 61.182
10. 5.6 x 7.6 = 42.56
14. 1.6 x 0.797 = 1.2752
3. 3.1 x 6.3 = 19.53
7. 2.2 x 9.49 = 20.878
11. 2.9 x 6.15 = 17.835
15. 0.72 x 5.79 = 4.1688
4. 2.9 x 1.5 = 4.35
8. 5.99 x 5.6 = 33.544
12. 8.6 x 5.8 = 49.88
16. 7.71 x 0.226 = 1.74246

59

page 59

Week 5 • Day 1
Parts of Speech

Know Your Word Types

In each sentence, decide whether the underlined word is a **noun** (N), **pronoun** (PN), **verb** (V), **adjective** (ADJ), **adverb** (ADV), **conjunction** (C), **preposition** (P), or **interjection** (I). Then write its abbreviation on the line before the sentence.

N 1. What is the world's most widely spoken language?
N 2. My soda can was extremely cold when I drank it.
ADJ 3. That large, extravagant home is overpriced for this neighborhood.
N 4. What is the difference between a hurricane and a storm?
I 5. Oh! I know how to complete that science experiment.
PN 6. She also enjoys cooking chicken dishes and delicious desserts.
ADJ 7. The dusty staircase in the old house made my aunt sneeze.
N 8. Dusty is our favorite horse on my grandfather's farm.
N 9. Hippos may look cute, but they are actually quite dangerous.
C 10. My dad is not a great singer, but I love him anyway.
V 11. When the phone rings, my sister runs to answer it.
N 12. The lady wore several rings on both of her hands.
ADV 13. The students sat quietly and listened to the teacher.
P 14. Sarah's puppy jumped over the bush and ran through the neighbor's garden.
ADV 15. Slowly the conductor directed his orchestra through the ballad.
N 16. Many restaurants serve salads with every entrée.

60

page 60

Week 5 • Day 2
Division

Divide & See What Remains

Find the quotients for the following division problems. Be sure to include the remainders in your answer.

1. 93 ÷ 45 = 2R3
2. 934 ÷ 15 = 62R4
3. 206 ÷ 17 = 12R2
4. 27 ÷ 13 = 2R1
5. 87 ÷ 33 = 2R21
6. 86 ÷ 82 = 1R4
7. 90 ÷ 7 = 12R6
8. 77 ÷ 2 = 38R1
9. 79 ÷ 13 = 6R1
10. 139 ÷ 14.7 = 9R13
11. 708 ÷ 7 = 101R1
12. 407 ÷ 23 = 17R16

61

page 61

Week 5 • Day 2
Parts of a Paragraph

Create a Paragraph

A **paragraph** *is a group of sentences that tells about one main idea.*
The **topic sentence** *tells the main idea and is usually the first sentence.*
Supporting sentences *tell more about the main idea.*
The **closing sentence** *of a paragraph often retells the main idea in a different way.*
Some paragraphs also have a **title**.

Here are the parts for one paragraph:

Paragraph Title	*Our Summer Vacation*
Topic Sentence	*The first day of our vacation was very disappointing.*
Supporting Sentences:	*1. It rained non-stop from sunrise to sunset.* *2. Thunder and lightning occurred all day long, so we had to stay indoors.* *3. The second day, we gladly went to the beach.* *4. The sky was blue, and the sun shone brightly.* *5. We built sand castles, went swimming and surfing.*
Closing Sentence	*The weather was perfect the rest of the week. I'm so glad I didn't go home after the first day!*

When you write a paragraph, remember the following rules:
- **Indent** *the first line so that readers know that you are beginning a paragraph.*
- **Capitalize** *the first word of each sentence.*
- **Punctuate** *each sentence correctly (. , ? !).*

Using all of the information above, rewrite the paragraph. Be sure to follow the rules.

Our Summer Vacation
paragraph title

The first day of our vacation was very disappointing. It rained non-stop from sunrise to sunset, and there was thunder and lightning all day, so we had to stay indoors. On the second day, we gladly went to the beach. The sky was blue and the sun shone brightly. We built sand castles and went swimming and surfing. The weather was perfect the rest of the week. I'm so glad I didn't go home after the first day!

62

page 62

Week 5 • Day 3
Converting Numbers

Working With Fractions, Decimals & Percents

Reduce these fractions to lowest terms. Circle the letter with the correct answer.

1. $\frac{9}{21}$ = A. $\frac{4}{10}$ B. $\frac{3}{8}$ **(C.)** $\frac{3}{7}$ D. $\frac{3}{12}$
2. $\frac{10}{18}$ = **(A.)** $\frac{5}{9}$ B. $\frac{2}{8}$ C. $\frac{5}{8}$ D. $\frac{2}{3}$
3. $\frac{11}{33}$ = A. $\frac{1}{5}$ B. $\frac{2}{11}$ C. $\frac{2}{3}$ **(D.)** $\frac{1}{3}$
4. $\frac{13}{39}$ = **(A.)** $\frac{1}{3}$ B. $\frac{1}{13}$ C. $\frac{4}{13}$ D. $\frac{7}{20}$

Compute the sums and differences of these decimals. Circle the letter with the correct answer.

5. **0.025 + 2.5 =** A. 2.552 **(B.)** 2.525 C. 2.535 D. 5.025
6. **5.1 + 0.384 =** **(A.)** 5.484 B. 5.44 C. 5.448 D. 5.584
7. **1 − 0.236 =** A. 0.1236 B. 0.00764 C. 1.746 **(D.)** 0.764
8. **7.444 + 3.666 =** **(A.)** 11.11 B. 111.11 C. 1.744 D. 10.11

Convert these decimals and fractions to percents. Circle the letter with the correct answer.

9. **0.25 =** A. 0.025% B. 2.5% **(C.)** 25% D. 0.25%
10. **0.33 =** **(A.)** 33% B. .033% C. 3.30% D. 330%
11. $\frac{1}{4}$ = A. 2.5% **(B.)** 25% C. 0.025% D. 0.25%
12. $\frac{3}{4}$ = **(A.)** 75% B. 750% C. 7.5% D. 0.75%

63

page 63

Week 5 • Day 3
Diagramming Sentences

A Picture of the Sentence

To diagram a sentence, first draw a long horizontal line. Then draw a short vertical line that crosses the horizontal line. Write the simple subject to the left of the vertical line. Write the simple predicate to the right of the vertical line. When diagramming sentences, use capital letters as they appear in the sentence, but do **not** use punctuation. *Diagramming a sentence is creating a picture of the sentence.*

Write only the **simple subject** and the **simple predicate** in the diagram.
Remember: The simple predicate can include a helping verb.

Example: The dynamite will explode on schedule. dynamite | will explode

Diagram only the simple subject and the simple predicate for each of the following sentences.

1. **Rodney went to the library.** Rodney | went
2. **Marsh threw the football.** Marsh | threw
3. **Today's special is baked tilapia.** special | is
4. **The heavy rainfall soaked the garden.** rainfall | soaked

In a sentence diagram, the **direct object** is placed to the right of the simple predicate. The vertical line before the direct object meets but does not cross the horizontal line.

Example: The library needs volunteers. library | needs | volunteers

Diagram the simple subject, predicate, and direct object.

5. **Fillipe finished the pizza.** Fillipe | finished | pizza
6. **Aunt Jenny bought the tickets.** Aunt Jenny | bought | tickets

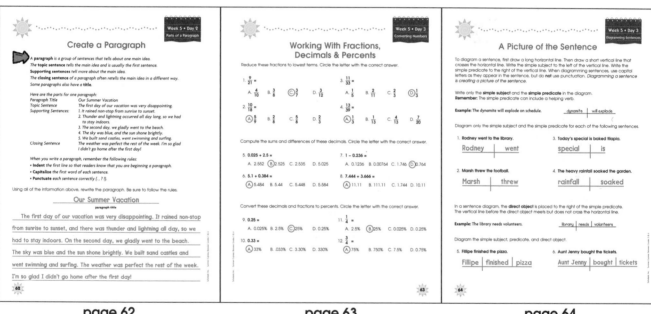

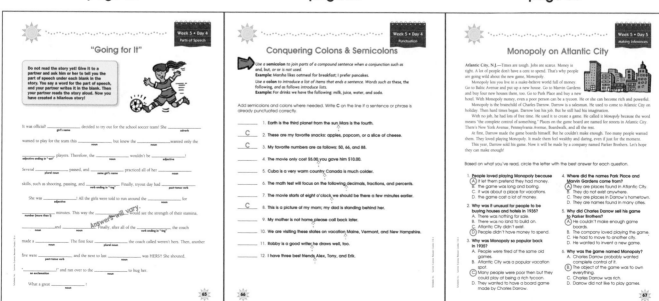

64

page 64

Week 5 • Day 4
Parts of Speech

"Going for It"

Do not read the story yet! Give it to a partner and ask him or her to tell you the part of speech under each blank in the story. You say a word for the part of speech, and your partner writes it in the blank. Then your partner reads the story aloud. Now you have created a hilarious story!

It was official! ________ (girl's name) decided to try out for the school soccer team! She ________ (adverb) wanted to play for the team this ________ (noun), but knew the ________ (noun) wanted only the ________ (adjective ending in "-est") players. Therefore, the ________ (noun) wouldn't be ________ (adjective)! Several ________ (plural noun) passed, and ________ (same girl's name) practiced all of her ________ (noun) skills, such as shooting, passing, and ________ (verb ending in "-ing"). Finally, tryout day had ________ (past-tense verb).

She was ________ (adjective)! All the girls were told to run around the ________ (noun) for ________ (number (more than 1)) minutes. This way the ________ (noun) would see the strength of their stamina, ________ (noun) and ________ (noun). Finally, after all of the ________ (verb ending in "-ing"), the coach made a ________ (noun). The first four ________ (plural noun) the coach called weren't hers. Then, another five were ________ (past-tense verb), and the next to last ________ (noun) was HERS!! She shouted, "________ (an exclamation)!" and ran over to the ________ (noun) to hug her.

What a great ________ (noun)!

Answers will vary.

65

page 65

Week 5 • Day 4
Punctuation

Conquering Colons & Semicolons

Use a **semicolon** *to join parts of a compound sentence when a conjunction such as* and, but, *or* or *is not used.*
Example: Marsha likes oatmeal for breakfast; I prefer pancakes.
Use a **colon** *to introduce a list of items that ends a sentence. Words such as* these, the following, *and* as follows *introduce lists.*
Example: For drinks we have the following: milk, juice, water, and soda.

Add semicolons and colons where needed. Write **C** on the line if a sentence or phrase is already punctuated correctly.

____ 1. Earth is the third planet from the sun; Mars is the fourth.
C 2. These are my favorite snacks: apples, popcorn, or a slice of cheese.
C 3. My favorite numbers are as follows: 50, 66, and 88.
____ 4. The movie only cost $5.00; you gave him $10.00.
____ 5. Cuba is a very warm country; Canada is much colder.
____ 6. The math test will focus on the following: decimals, fractions, and percents.
____ 7. The movie starts at eight o'clock; we should be there a few minutes earlier.
C 8. This is a picture of my mom; my dad is standing behind her.
____ 9. My mother is not home; please call back later.
____ 10. We are visiting these states on vacation: Maine, Vermont, and New Hampshire.
____ 11. Robby is a good writer; he draws well, too.
____ 12. I have three best friends: Alex, Tony, and Erik.

66

page 66

Week 5 • Day 5
Making Inferences

Monopoly on Atlantic City

Atlantic City, N.J.—Times are tough. Jobs are scarce. Money is tight. A lot of people don't have a cent to spend. That's why people are going wild about the new game, Monopoly.

Monopoly lets you live in a make-believe world full of money. Go to Baltic Avenue and put up a new house. Go to Marvin Gardens and buy four new houses there, too. Go to Park Place and buy a new hotel. With Monopoly money, even a poor person can be a tycoon. He or she can become rich and powerful.

Monopoly is the brainchild of Charles Darrow. Darrow is a salesman. He used to come to Atlantic City on holiday. Then hard times began. Darrow lost his job. But he still had his imagination.

With no job, he had lots of free time. He used it to create a game. He called it *Monopoly* because the word means "the complete control of something." Places on the game board are named for streets in Atlantic City. There's New York Avenue, Pennsylvania Avenue, Boardwalk, and all the rest.

At first, Darrow made the game boards himself. But he couldn't make enough. Too many people wanted them. They loved playing Monopoly. It made them feel wealthy and daring, even if just for the moment.

This year, Darrow sold his game. Now it will be made by a company named Parker Brothers. Let's hope they can make enough!

Based on what you've read, circle the letter with the best answer for each question.

1. **People loved playing Monopoly because**
   - **(A.)** it let them pretend they had money.
   - B. the game was long and boring.
   - C. it was about a place for vacations.
   - D. the game cost a lot of money.
2. **Why was it unusual for people to be buying houses and hotels in 1935?**
   - A. There was nothing for sale.
   - B. There was no land to build on.
   - C. Atlantic City didn't exist.
   - **(D.)** People didn't have money to spend.
3. **Why was Monopoly so popular back in 1935?**
   - A. People were tired of the same old games.
   - B. Atlantic City was a popular vacation spot.
   - **(C.)** Many people were poor then but they could play at being a rich tycoon.
   - D. They wanted to have a board game made by Charles Darrow.
4. **Where did the names Park Place and Marvin Gardens come from?**
   - **(A.)** They are places found in Atlantic City.
   - B. They do not exist anywhere.
   - C. They are places in Darrow's hometown.
   - D. They are names found in many cities.
5. **Why did Charles Darrow sell his game to Parker Brothers?**
   - **(A.)** He couldn't make enough game boards.
   - B. The company loved playing the game.
   - C. He had to move to another city.
   - D. He wanted to invent a new game.
6. **Why was the game named Monopoly?**
   - A. Charles Darrow probably wanted complete control of it.
   - **(B.)** The object of the game was to own everything.
   - C. Charles Darrow was rich.
   - D. Darrow did not like to play games.

67

page 67

Week 5 • Day 5
Reading for Understanding

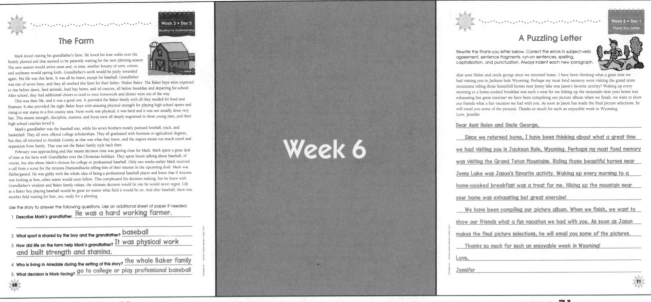

The Farm

Mark loved visiting his grandfather's farm. He loved his lone walks over the freshly plowed soil that seemed to be patiently waiting for the next planting season. The new season would arrive soon and, in time, another bounty of corn, cotton, and soybeans would spring forth. Grandfather's work would be justly rewarded again. His life was this farm. It was all he knew, except for baseball. Grandfather was one of seven boys, and they all worked this farm for their father, Walter Baker. The Baker boys were expected to rise before dawn, feed animals, load hay barns, and oil tractors, all before breakfast and departing for school. After school, they had additional chores to tend to once homework and dinner were out of the way.

This was their life, and it was a good one. It provided the Baker family with all they needed for food and finances. It also provided the eight Baker boys with amazing physical strength for playing high school sports and rising to star status in a five-county area. Farm work was physical; it was hard and it was not usually done very fast. This meant strength, discipline, stamina, and focus were all deeply engrained in these young men, and their high school coaches loved it.

Mark's grandfather was the baseball star, while his seven brothers mostly pursued football, track, and basketball. They all were offered college scholarships. They all graduated with business or agriculture degrees, but they all returned to Airedale County as that was what they knew, and the majors meant too much travel and separation from family. That was not the Baker family style back then.

February was approaching and that meant decision time was getting close for Mark. Mark spent a great deal of time at the farm with Grandfather over the Christmas holidays. They spent hours talking about baseball, of course, but also about Mark's choices for college or professional baseball. Only two weeks earlier Mark received a call from a scout for the Arizona Diamondbacks telling him of their interest in the upcoming draft. Mark was flabbergasted. He was giddy with the whole idea of being a professional baseball player and knew that if Arizona was looking at him, other teams would soon follow. This complicated his decision making, but he knew with Grandfather's wisdom and Baker family values, the ultimate decision would be one he would never regret. Life as a Baker boy playing baseball would be great no matter what field it would be on. And after baseball, there was another field waiting for him, too, ready for a planting.

Use the story to answer the following questions. Use an additional sheet of paper if needed.

1. **Describe Mark's grandfather.** He was a hard working farmer.
2. **What sport is shared by the boy and the grandfather?** baseball
3. **How did life on the farm help Mark's grandfather?** It was physical work and built strength and stamina.
4. **Who is living in Airedale during the setting of this story?** the whole Baker family
5. **What decision is Mark facing?** go to college or play professional baseball

68

page 68

Week 6

Week 6 • Day 1
Thank-You Letter

A Puzzling Letter

Rewrite the thank-you letter below. Correct the errors in subject-verb agreement, sentence fragments, run-on sentences, spelling, capitalization, and punctuation. Always indent each new paragraph.

dear aunt Helen and uncle george since we returned home. I have been thinking what a great time we had visiting you in Jackson hole Wyoming. Perhaps my most fond memory were visiting the grand teton mountains riding those beautifull horses near Jenny lake was Jason's favorite activity? Waking up every morning to a home-cooked breakfast was such a treat for me hiking up the mountain near your home was exhausting but great exercise! we have been compileing our picture album when we finish, we want to show our friends what a fun vacation we had with you. As soon as Jason has made the final picture selections, he will email you some of the pictures. Thanks so much for such an enjoyable week in Wyoming.
Love, Jennifer

Dear Aunt Helen and Uncle George,

Since we returned home, I have been thinking about what a great time we had visiting you in Jackson Hole, Wyoming. Perhaps my most fond memory was visiting the Grand Teton Mountains. Riding those beautiful horses near Jenny Lake was Jason's favorite activity. Waking up every morning to a home-cooked breakfast was a treat for me. Hiking up the mountain near your home was exhausting but great exercise!

We have been compiling our picture album. When we finish, we want to show our friends what a fun vacation we had with you. As soon as Jason makes the final picture selections, he will email you some of the pictures.

Thanks so much for such an enjoyable week in Wyoming!

Love,

Jennifer

71

page 71

Week 6 • Day 1
Basic Operations

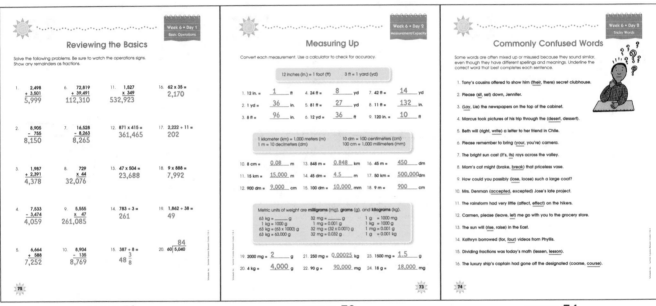

Reviewing the Basics

Solve the following problems. Be sure to watch the operations signs. Show any remainders as fractions.

1. 2,498 + 3,501 = 5,999
2. 8,905 − 755 = 8,150
3. 1,987 + 2,391 = 4,378
4. 7,533 − 3,474 = 4,059
5. 6,664 + 588 = 7,252
6. 72,819 + 39,491 = 112,310
7. 16,528 − 8,263 = 8,265
8. 729 x 44 = 32,076
9. 5,555 x 47 = 261,085
10. 8,904 − 135 = 8,769
11. 1,527 x 349 = 532,923
12. 871 x 415 = 361,465
13. 47 x 504 = 23,688
14. 783 ÷ 3 = 261
15. 387 ÷ 8 = $48\frac{3}{8}$
16. 62 x 35 = 2,170
17. 2,222 ÷ 11 = 202
18. 9 x 888 = 7,992
19. 1,862 ÷ 38 = 49
20. 5,040 ÷ 60 = 84

72

page 72

Week 6 • Day 2
Measurement/Capacity

Measuring Up

Convert each measurement. Use a calculator to check for accuracy.

12 inches (in.) = 1 foot (ft) 3 ft = 1 yard (yd)

1. 12 in. = 1 ft
2. 1 yd = 36 in.
3. 8 ft = 96 in.
4. 24 ft = 8 yd
5. 81 ft = 27 yd
6. 12 yd = 36 ft
7. 42 ft = 14 yd
8. 11 ft = 132 in.
9. 120 in. = 10 ft

1 kilometer (km) = 1,000 meters (m)
1 m = 10 decimeters (dm)
10 dm = 100 centimeters (cm)
100 cm = 1,000 millimeters (mm)

10. 8 cm = 0.08 m
11. 15 km = 15,000 m
12. 900 dm = 9,000 cm
13. 848 m = 0.848 km
14. 45 dm = 4.5 m
15. 100 dm = 10,000 mm
16. 45 m = 450 dm
17. 50 km = 500,000 dm
18. 9 m = 900 cm

Metric units of weight are **milligrams** (mg), **grams** (g), and **kilograms** (kg).

63 kg = ____ g	32 mg = ____ g	1 g = 1000 mg
1 kg = 1000 g	1 mg = 0.001 g	1 kg = 1000 g
63 kg = (63 x 1000) g	32 mg = (32 x 0.001) g	1 mg = 0.001 g
63 kg = 63,000 g	32 mg = 0.032 g	1 g = 0.001 kg

19. 2000 mg = 2 g
20. 4 kg = 4,000 g
21. 250 mg = 0.00025 kg
22. 90 g = 90,000 mg
23. 1500 mg = 1.5 g
24. 18 g = 18,000 mg

73

page 73

Week 6 • Day 2
Tricky Words

Commonly Confused Words

Some words are often mixed up or misused because they sound similar, even though they have different spellings and meanings. Underline the correct word that best completes each sentence.

1. Tony's cousins offered to show him (their, there) secret clubhouse.
2. Please (sit, set) down, Jennifer.
3. (Lay, Lie) the newspapers on the top of the cabinet.
4. Marcus took pictures of his trip through the (desert, dessert).
5. Beth will (right, write) a letter to her friend in Chile.
6. Please remember to bring (your, you're) camera.
7. The bright sun cast (it's, its) rays across the valley.
8. Mom's cat might (brake, break) that priceless vase.
9. How could you possibly (lose, loose) such a large coat?
10. Mrs. Denman (accepted, excepted) Jose's late project.
11. The rainstorm had very little (affect, effect) on the hikers.
12. Carmen, please (leave, let) me go with you to the grocery store.
13. The sun will (rise, raise) in the East.
14. Kathryn borrowed (for, four) videos from Phyllis.
15. Dividing fractions was today's math (lessen, lesson).
16. The luxury ship's captain had gone off the designated (coarse, course).

74

page 74

Week 6 • Day 3
Geometric Concepts

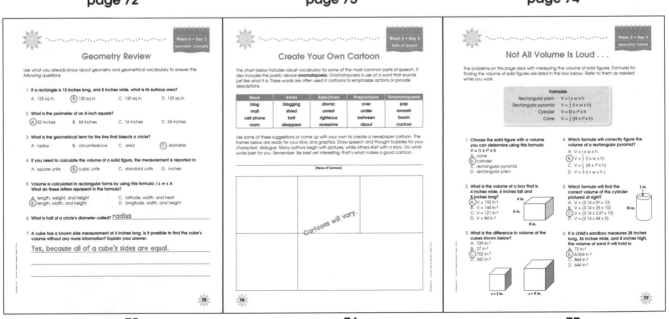

Geometry Review

Use what you already know about geometry and geometrical vocabulary to answer the following questions.

1. **If a rectangle is 15 inches long, and 8 inches wide, what is its surface area?**
   A. 125 sq in. (B.) 120 sq in. C. 130 sq in. D. 135 sq in.
2. **What is the perimeter of an 8-inch square?**
   (A.) 32 inches B. 64 inches C. 16 inches D. 24 inches
3. **What is the geometrical term for the line that bisects a circle?**
   A. radius B. circumference C. area (D.) diameter
4. **If you need to calculate the volume of a solid figure, the measurement is reported in:**
   A. square units (B.) cubic units C. standard units D. inches
5. **Volume is calculated in rectangular forms by using this formula: *l* x *w* x *h*. What do these letters represent in the formula?**
   A. length, weight, and height
   (B.) length, width, and height
   C. latitude, width, and heat
   D. longitude, width, and height
6. **What is half of a circle's diameter called?** radius
7. **A cube has a known side measurement of 4 inches long. Is it possible to find the cube's volume without any more information? Explain your answer.**
   Yes, because all of a cube's sides are equal.

75

page 75

Week 6 • Day 3
Parts of Speech

Create Your Own Cartoon

The chart below includes robust vocabulary for some of the most common parts of speech. It also includes the poetic device **onomatopoeia**. Onomatopoeia is use of a word that sounds just like what it is. These words are often used in cartoons to emphasize actions or provide descriptions.

Noun	Verbs	Adjectives	Prepositions	Onomatopoeia
blog	blogging	atomic	over	pop
mall	shred	unreal	under	swoosh
cell phone	bolt	righteous	between	boom
mom	disappear	awesome	about	cuckoo

Use some of these suggestions or come up with your own to create a newspaper cartoon. The frames below are ready for your story and graphics. Draw speech and thought bubbles for your characters' dialogue. Many authors begin with pictures, while others start with a story. Do what works best for you. Remember: Be brief yet interesting; that's what makes a good cartoon.

(Name of Cartoon)

Cartoons will vary.

76

page 76

Week 6 • Day 4
Measuring Volume

Not All Volume Is Loud . . .

The problems on this page deal with measuring the volume of solid figures. Formulas for finding the volume of solid figures are listed in the box below. Refer to them as needed while you work.

Formulas

Rectangular prism	$V = l \times w \times h$
Rectangular pyramid	$V = \frac{1}{3}(l \times w \times h)$
Cylinder	$V = \Pi \times r^2 \times h$
Cone	$V = \frac{1}{3}(\Pi \times r^2 \times h)$

1. **Choose the solid figure with a volume you can determine using this formula: $V = \Pi \times r^2 \times h$**
   A. cone
   (B.) cylinder
   C. rectangular pyramid
   D. rectangular prism
2. **What is the volume of a box that is 4 inches wide, 6 inches tall and 8 inches long?**
   (A.) $V = 192$ in.^{3}
   B. $V = 144$ in.^{3}
   C. $V = 121$ in.^{3}
   D. $V = 84$ in.^{3}

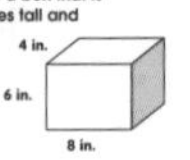

4 in.
6 in.
8 in.

3. **What is the difference in volume of the cubes shown below?**
   A. 729 in.^{3}
   B. 27 in.^{3}
   (C.) 702 in.^{3}
   D. 360 in.^{3}

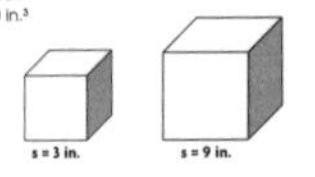

s = 3 in.
s = 9 in.

4. **Which formula will correctly figure the volume of a rectangular pyramid?**
   A. $V = l \times w \times h$
   (B.) $V = \frac{1}{3}(l \times w \times h)$
   C. $V = \frac{1}{3}(\Pi \times r^2 \times h)$
   D. $V = 3(l \times w \times h)$
5. **Which formula will find the correct volume of the cylinder pictured at right?**
   A. $V = (3.14 \times 5^2 \times 10)$
   B. $V = (3.14 \times 25 \times 10)$
   (C.) $V = (3.14 \times 2.5^2 \times 10)$
   D. $V = (3.14 \times 44 \times 5)$

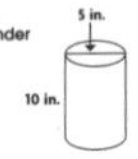

5 in.
10 in.

6. **If a child's sandbox measures 28 inches long, 36 inches wide, and 8 inches high, the volume of sand it will hold is:**
   A. 72 in.^{3}
   (B.) 8,064 in.^{3}
   C. 864 in.^{3}
   D. 644 in.^{3}

77

page 77

Week 6 • Day 4
Research Skills

Electronic Reference Sources

Challenge a friend or family member to answer the following Science Trivia questions, or do this exercise by using the Internet, an online encyclopedia, or trustworthy database site.

1. How many minutes does it take the average person to fall asleep? 7 minutes
2. What is the largest venomous snake? King Cobra
3. What is the human bone most frequently broken? collar bone
4. Do mosquitoes have teeth? yes
5. What is the base unit of mass in the metric system? kilogram
6. What is the little ridge between your nose and upper lip called? philtrum
7. What is the opening at the top of a volcano called? crater
8. What computer was introduced in the 1984 Super Bowl ads? the Macintosh
9. How many calories are in a glass of water? 0
10. What is the most common blood type? O
11. What is the fastest reptile on land? spiny-tailed iguana
12. What method of underwater detection is short for "sound navigation and ranging"? sonar
13. What substance earns recyclers the most money? aluminum
14. What planet is the brightest object in the sky after the sun and moon? Venus
15. What liquid metal was commonly used in thermometers? mercury

page 78

Week 6 • Day 5
Word Problems

Fraction Fun

Solve each fraction word problem. Then circle the best answer. Be sure to show your work.

1. Ryan has $17\frac{3}{8}$ yards of coated wire for his zip line. He used $8\frac{1}{4}$ yards to section off the ride area between 2 trees. How many yards of wire does he have left?

   A. $7\frac{5}{8}$ (B.) $9\frac{1}{8}$ C. $10\frac{1}{8}$ D. $21\frac{5}{8}$

2. It takes 4 hours to clean the Eubanks' condo. How many hours does it take to clean $\frac{7}{8}$ of it?

   (A.) $3\frac{1}{2}$ B. $3\frac{3}{4}$ C. $2\frac{4}{9}$ D. $3\frac{1}{8}$

3. Mr. Palter purchased 30 blank rewritable CDs. He placed $\frac{1}{5}$ of the CDs in his briefcase. How many CDs did Mr. Palter pack in his briefcase?

   A. 5 B. 12 (C.) 6 D. 60

4. Maria made 3 dresses for the Greek Festival dance. She used $6\frac{3}{8}$ yards of fabric for all 3 dresses. If she adds $2\frac{3}{8}$ yards of trim to the dresses, how many total yards of material will she use?

   A. $10\frac{1}{4}$ (B.) $9\frac{3}{8}$ C. $7\frac{5}{8}$ D. $9\frac{3}{4}$

5. John has $\frac{1}{2}$ of a pizza left in the fridge. For breakfast he ate $\frac{1}{3}$ of it. What fraction of that does he have left?

   A. $\frac{5}{6}$ B. $\frac{2}{3}$ C. $\frac{2}{5}$ (D.) $\frac{1}{6}$

6. The 8th grade orchestra performed 3 songs at the concert. The first song was $3\frac{3}{4}$ minutes long. The next song was $5\frac{1}{4}$ minutes long. The last song was $4\frac{1}{2}$ minutes. How many minutes did the orchestra play in all?

   (A.) $13\frac{1}{2}$ B. $12\frac{3}{4}$ C. $11\frac{1}{4}$ D. $14\frac{1}{2}$

page 79

Week 6 • Day 5
Topic Sentences

Creating a Topic Sentence

Commonly appearing at (or near) the beginning of a paragraph, a **topic sentence** expresses the main idea of the paragraph. What usually follows are sentences that develop the main idea with specific details. Using the information given in each paragraph below, create a topic sentence that will interest readers, then write it on the line provided.

Answers will vary. Possible topic sentences are shown.

1. Mount Everest is 29,079 feet (8,863 meters) above sea level. It is part of the Himalayan range in South Asia. Despite its awesome height, the mountain has been climbed many times. Sir Edmund Hillary and his guide, Tenzing Norgay, were the first to climb the mountain, reaching the summit on May 29, 1953. Mount Everest attracts well-experienced mountaineers as well as novice climbers who are willing to pay substantial sums to professional mountain guides to complete a successful climb.

   Mt. Everest is the highest place on earth.

2. Harriet Tubman was an African-American spy for the Union Army during the American Civil War. After escaping from slavery, into which she was born, Tubman made 13 missions, rescuing over 70 slaves, via a network of antislavery activists and safe houses known as the Underground Railroad. She traveled by night in extreme secrecy. Harriet (or "Moses," as she was called) never lost a passenger. Large rewards were offered for the capture and return of many of the people she helped escape; however, no one ever knew it was Harriet Tubman who was helping them.

   Harriet Tubman was an Underground Railroad operator, antislavery activist, and Civil War spy.

3. Alligators and crocodiles have been considered villainous, man-eating monsters for centuries, but this was not always the case. Many tall tales have been told about these giant reptiles with long tails. This is partly due to the fact that crocodiles and alligators have truly ancient roots, going all the way back to when dinosaurs still roamed the earth. The two reptiles are often confused, but visually crocodiles and alligators are quite different. Alligators have a very broad, wide snout, and crocodiles have a narrower snout and jaw.

   Alligators and crocodiles have fascinated people for ages.

4. Hoover Dam, once known as Boulder Dam, is a concrete, arch-gravity dam in the Black Canyon of the Colorado River. The dam is located on the border between Arizona and Nevada. It was constructed between 1931 and 1936 and dedicated on September 30, 1935 by President Franklin Roosevelt. The dam is 726 feet high and 1,244 feet wide. Hoover Dam was actually built to help the farmers in Arizona, Nevada, and southern California. For years, the farmers were flooded once a year. The dam was built to stop the floods and also provide electricity for Arizona, Nevada, and part of California.

   The Hoover Dam helps farmers, residents, and businesses in many ways.

page 80

Week 7

Week 7 • Day 1
Persuasive Writing

Letter to the Editor

Below is a letter to the editor from a reader who wanted to share a difference of opinion. The letter contains sentences that give strong reasons and valid attempts at persuading the reader to change his or her beliefs. There are also some weak sentences that would not compel a reader to change his or her opinion. On the lines below, list the sentences you find most persuasive.

Dear Editor:

I am writing about an article entitled "Sidewalk Success," which appeared in the January 27th edition of *The Sun Valley Times*. Your reporter described our city's current "operation sidewalk" project as a gift to all of the citizens and stated it would begin in February. It is now March, and nothing is being done to begin this project. There have even been television reports stating the funds are not able to completely cover the cost of the project. I believe you should print a corrected version of this sidewalk story to properly report on the true details of this project.

First, a gift is transferred to another person at no cost to the one receiving it; so these sidewalks are not "gifts." Also, the project needs more time to be done. Proper sidewalk construction takes two weeks to complete, but your reporter stated the entire project will only require ten weeks for nine sidewalks. That is mathematically impossible. Additionally, the project is targeted to help schools and shopping centers, but your reporter did not mention that at all.

There are no flowerbeds at the entrances of Mill Glenn Drive, Applegate Road, and Tilly Pond Street because these areas are waiting for sidewalks. Your reporter did not seem to care about the speed of this project and how a quick and efficient process would help everyone. I would appreciate it if your staff would consider reporting on this project again, and in a truthful and complete manner for the citizens of our town.

Best regards,

Tim W.
Sun Valley, Idaho

On the lines below, list the points you believe the writer makes in this letter that are most persuasive.

Answers will vary.

page 83

Week 7 • Day 1
Roman Numerals

Roman Numerals—As Easy as I, II, III

Convert the numbers. The first one has been done for you.

I = 1 V = 5 X = 10 L = 50 C = 100 D = 500 M = 1,000

1. DCCCXLII = 842
2. MDCXI = 1611
3. MDCXLVIII = 1648
4. 1698 = MDCXCVIII
5. MMCLXXIV = 2174
6. CMLXIX = 969
7. MCCCXVII = 1317
8. 62 = LXII
9. MCDXL = 1440
10. MMDCCCLXX = 2870
11. 882 = DCCCLXXXII
12. DXXXIV = 534
13. 993 = CMXCIII
14. MMCDLXXXIX = 2489
15. DCLIII = 653

Complete the following addition and subtraction problems. The first one has been done for you.

16. LVI + V = 61, LXI
17. XLV – VIII = 37, XXXVII
18. LXXIV + LXII = 136, CXXXVI

page 84

Week 7 • Day 2
Main Idea

Identifying the Main Idea

Read the following passage and answer the questions at the bottom of this page. Pay close attention to the main ideas that are presented in each of the three paragraphs.

The Ming Dynasty

The Ming Dynasty was the ruling dynasty of China from 1368 to 1644. This dynasty, regarded as an era of social stability and orderly government, was the last dynasty in China ruled by the Hans, an ethnic group of Chinese people, perhaps the largest ethnic group in the world. The Ming capital of Beijing fell to a rebellion in 1644, and was succeeded by the Shun and Qing dynasties. The Ming is recognized for its numerous accomplishments, including the establishment of a major navy, an army of one million troops, and flourishing maritime trade. There were enormous construction projects, too, most notably the building of the Great Wall, restoration of the Grand Canal, and creation of the Forbidden City in Beijing.

Because of its many achievements, the Ming Dynasty is considered a high point in Chinese civilization. It is also an era in which the first signs of capitalism emerged in China. The ruling classes as well as people in rural and urban areas experienced great changes—many that were unanticipated and unintended. The great Emperor Hongwu wanted to build a fixed, immobile society of self-sufficient, rural communities that would have no need to interact with urban centers. However, the build-up of China's agricultural base and establishment of strong communication routes due to a militarized courier system had an unintended effect: it created an agricultural surplus, and this supply of goods could be sold at the growing markets all along courier routes. Communication and trade increased and rural regions and commerce were influenced by urban trends.

The upper levels of society, primarily the scholarly-gentry class, were also affected by this new trend toward a consumer culture. Traditionally only the family members of the scholarly class would take the exams to become scholar-officials; but now merchant families offered their own exam candidates and began to assume the cultural practices typical of the gentry. This trend toward change in social class and commercialism was not an isolated one; there were also changes in political and social philosophy, and in arts and literature. Answers will vary but should reflect the following:

1. What is the main idea of the first paragraph? The Ming dynasty is regarded as an era of stability and order and is recognized for its many achievements.
2. What is the main idea of the second paragraph? The Ming dynasty is considered a high point in Chinese civilization and brought about great changes.
3. What is the main idea of the third paragraph? Consumer culture changed society, politics, philosophy, art, and culture.

page 85

Week 7 • Day 2
Dictionary Skills

Look It Up!

Match each word with its definition. You may use a dictionary, a science book, or the Internet.

E 1. **asteroids** A. A celestial body that travels in an orbit around a planet or moon
H 2. **crater** B. The cutting off of light from one celestial body by another
B 3. **eclipse** C. A vent in the planetary surface through which magma and associated gases and ash erupt
G 4. **igneous** D. The luminous phenomenon seen when a meteoroid enters the atmosphere, commonly known as a shooting star
D 5. **meteor** E. Any of numerous small, often irregularly shaped bodies that orbit the sun, chiefly in the region of Mars and Jupiter
I 6. **planet** F. The layer of the earth's atmosphere that lies above the troposphere and below the mesosphere
A 7. **satellite** G. Rock or mineral that solidified from molten or partly molten material
F 8. **stratosphere** H. A depression formed by the impact of a meteorite, or a depression around the orifice of a volcano
C 9. **volcano** I. The large, spherical body made of rocks and ice orbiting the sun or another star
J 10. **weight** J. The gravitational force exerted on an object

Write the words in the box below in alphabetical order on the lines provided.

protrude	aggressive	morsel	gorge
sluggish	slither	accommodate	bask
conceal	flail	carcass	ripple

1. accommodate
2. aggressive
3. bask
4. carcass
5. conceal
6. flail
7. gorge
8. morsel
9. protrude
10. ripple
11. slither
12. sluggish

page 86

Week 7 • Day 3
Symmetry

Shapes in Motion

Look at each pair of figures to decide if they are congruent or similar. Write *similar* or *congruent* below each pair of figures. (To be congruent, the shapes must coincide at all points when one is placed over the other.) Next, find the line or lines of symmetry for each of the figures by drawing a line at each line of symmetry.

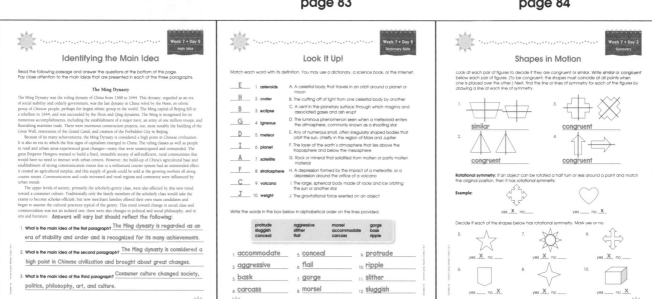

1. 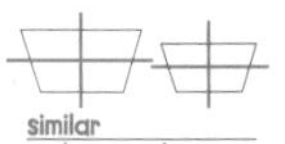
similar

2. 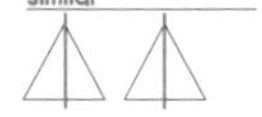
congruent

3. 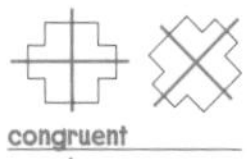
congruent

4. 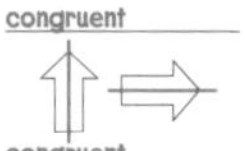
congruent

Rotational symmetry: If an object can be rotated a half turn or less around a point and match the original position, then it has *rotational symmetry*.

Example:

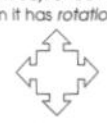
yes X no ___

yes ___ no X

Decide if each of the shapes below has rotational symmetry. Mark yes or no.

5. 
yes X no ___

6. 
yes ___ no X

7. 
yes X no ___

8. 
yes X no ___

9. 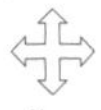
yes X no ___

10. 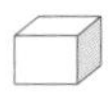
yes ___ no X

page 87

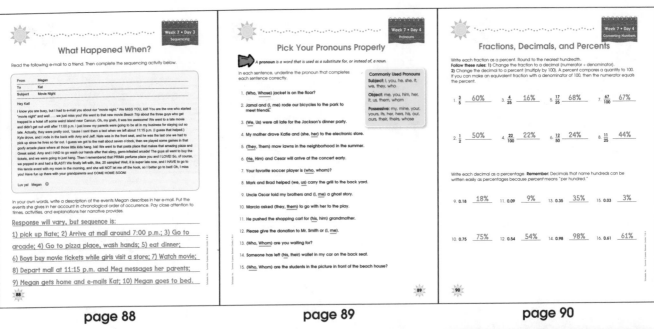

page 88   page 89   page 90

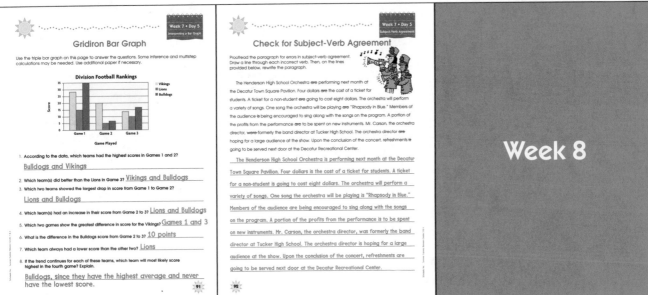

page 91   page 92

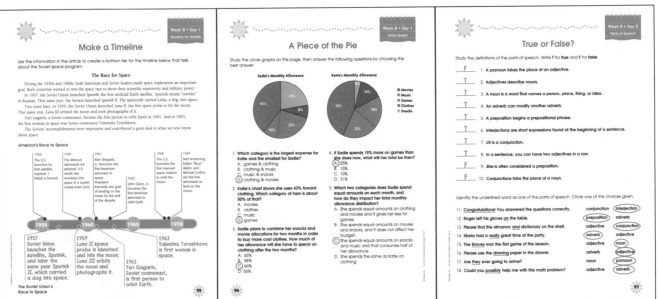

page 95   page 96   page 97

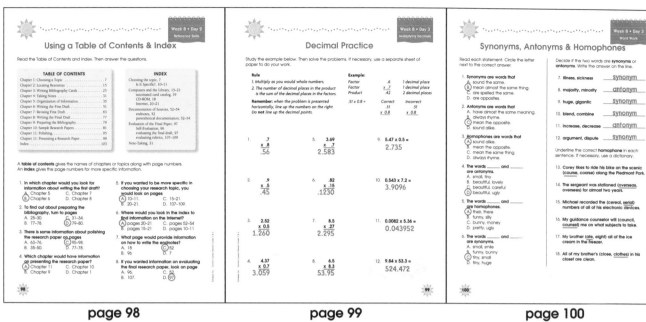

Week 8 • Day 2
Reference Skills

Using a Table of Contents & Index

Read the Table of Contents and Index. Then answer the questions.

TABLE OF CONTENTS

INDEX

A **table of contents** gives the names of chapters or topics along with page numbers. An **index** gives the page numbers for more specific information.

1. **In which chapter would you look for information about writing the first draft?**
A. Chapter 5 C. Chapter 7
B. Chapter 6 D. Chapter 8

2. **To find out about preparing the bibliography, turn to pages**
A. 25–30. C. 31–34.
B. 77–78. D. 79–80.

3. **There is some information about polishing the research paper on pages**
A. 63–76. C. 95–98.
B. 35–50. D. 77–78.

4. **Which chapter would have information on presenting the research paper?**
A. Chapter 11 C. Chapter 10
B. Chapter 9 D. Chapter 1

5. **If you wanted to be more specific in choosing your research topic, you would look on pages**
A. 10–11. C. 15–21.
B. 20–21. D. 107–109.

6. **Where would you look in the index to find information on the Internet?**
A. pages 20–21 C. pages 52–54
B. pages 15–21 D. pages 10–11

7. **What page would provide information on how to write the endnotes?**
A. 18 C. 52
B. 96 D. 7

8. **If you wanted information on evaluating the final research paper, look on page**
A. 96. C. 52.
B. 107. D. 97

98

page 98

Week 8 • Day 3
Multiplying Decimals

Decimal Practice

Study the example below. Then solve the problems. If necessary, use a separate sheet of paper to do your work.

Rule

1. Multiply as you would whole numbers.
2. The number of decimal places in the product is the sum of the decimal places in the factors.

Remember: *when the problem is presented horizontally, line up the numbers on the right. Do* **not** *line up the decimal points.*

Example:

Factor	*.6*	*1 decimal place*
Factor	*x .7*	*1 decimal place*
Product	*.42*	*2 decimal places*

.51 x 0.8 = *Correct* *.51 x 0.8* *Incorrect* *.51 x 0.8*

1. .7 x .8 = .56
2. .9 x .5 = .45
3. 2.52 x 0.5 = 1.260
4. 4.37 x 0.7 = 3.059
5. 3.69 x .7 = 2.583
6. .82 x .15 = .1230
7. 8.5 x .27 = 2.295
8. 6.5 x 8.3 = 53.95
9. **5.47 x 0.5 =** 2.735
10. **0.543 x 7.2 =** 3.9096
11. **0.0082 x 5.36 =** 0.043952
12. **9.84 x 53.3 =** 524.472

99

page 99

Week 8 • Day 3
Word Work

Synonyms, Antonyms & Homophones

Read each statement. Circle the letter next to the correct answer.

1. **Synonyms are words that**
A. sound the same.
B. mean almost the same thing.
C. are spelled the same.
D. are opposites.

2. **Antonyms are words that**
A. have almost the same meaning.
B. always rhyme.
C. mean the opposite.
D. sound alike.

3. **Homophones are words that**
A. sound alike.
B. mean the opposite.
C. mean the same thing.
D. always rhyme.

4. **The words _____ and _____ are antonyms.**
A. small, tiny
B. beautiful, lovely
C. beautiful, careful
D. beautiful, ugly

5. **The words _____ and _____ are homophones.**
A. their, there
B. funny, silly
C. bunny, money
D. pretty, ugly

6. **The words _____ and _____ are synonyms.**
A. small, smile
B. funny, bunny
C. tiny, small
D. tiny, huge

Decide if the two words are **synonyms** or **antonyms**. Write the answer on the line.

7. **illness, sickness** synonym
8. **majority, minority** antonym
9. **huge, gigantic** synonym
10. **blend, combine** synonym
11. **increase, decrease** antonym
12. **argument, dispute** synonym

Underline the correct **homophone** in each sentence. If necessary, use a dictionary.

13. **Corey likes to ride his bike on the scenic (course, coarse) along the Piedmont Park.**
14. **The sergeant was stationed (overseas, oversees) for almost two years.**
15. **Michael recorded the (cereal, serial) numbers of all of his electronic devices.**
16. **My guidance counselor will (council, counsel) me on what subjects to take.**
17. **My brother (ate, eight) all of the ice cream in the freezer.**
18. **All of my brother's (close, clothes) in his closet are clean.**

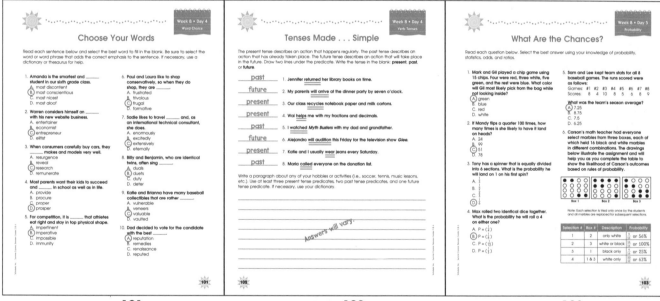

100

page 100

Week 8 • Day 4
Word Choice

Choose Your Words

Read each sentence below and select the best word to fill in the blank. Be sure to select the word or word phrase that adds the correct emphasis to the sentence. If necessary, use a dictionary or thesaurus for help.

1. **Amanda is the smartest and _____ student in our sixth grade class.**
A. most discontent
B. most conscientious
C. most nicest
D. most aloof

2. **Warren considers himself an _____ with his new website business.**
A. entertainer
B. economist
C. entrepreneur
D. elitist

3. **When consumers carefully buy cars, they _____ makes and models very well.**
A. resurgence
B. reveal
C. research
D. remunerate

4. **Most parents want their kids to succeed and _____ in school as well as in life.**
A. provide
B. procure
C. proper
D. prosper

5. **For competition, it is _____ that athletes eat right and stay in top physical shape.**
A. impertinent
B. imperative
C. impossible
D. immunity

6. **Paul and Laura like to shop conservatively, so when they do shop, they are _____.**
A. frustrated
B. frivolous
C. frugal
D. formative

7. **Sadie likes to travel _____ and, as an international technical consultant, she does.**
A. enormously
B. excitedly
C. extensively
D. eternally

8. **Billy and Benjamin, who are identical twins, often sing _____.**
A. duals
B. duets
C. duty
D. deter

9. **Katie and Brianna have many baseball collectibles that are rather _____.**
A. vulnerable
B. veneers
C. valuable
D. vaulted

10. **Dad decided to vote for the candidate with the best _____.**
A. reputation
B. remedies
C. renaissance
D. reputed

101

page 101

Week 8 • Day 4
Verb Tenses

Tenses Made . . . Simple

The present tense describes an action that happens regularly. The past tense describes an action that has already taken place. The future tense describes an action that will take place in the future. Draw two lines under the predicate. Write the tense in the blank: **present**, **past**, or **future**.

past 1. **Jennifer returned her library books on time.**
future 2. **My parents will arrive at the dinner party by seven o'clock.**
present 3. **Our class recycles notebook paper and milk cartons.**
present 4. **Wai helps me with my fractions and decimals.**
past 5. **I watched *Myth Busters* with my dad and grandfather.**
future 6. **Alejandro will audition this Friday for the television show *Glee*.**
present 7. **Katie and I usually wear jeans every Saturday.**
past 8. **Maria called everyone on the donation list.**

Write a paragraph about any of your hobbies or activities (i.e., soccer, tennis, music lessons, etc.). Use at least three present tense predicates, two past tense predicates, and one future tense predicate. If necessary, use your dictionary.

Answers will vary.

102

page 102

Week 8 • Day 5
Probability

What Are the Chances?

Read each question below. Select the best answer using your knowledge of probability, statistics, odds, and ratios.

1. **Mark and Gil played a chip game using 15 chips. Four were red, three white, five green, and the rest were blue. What color will Gil most likely pick from the bag while not looking inside?**
A. green
B. blue
C. red
D. white

2. **If Mandy flips a quarter 100 times, how many times is she likely to have it land on heads?**
A. 24
B. 99
C. 51
D. 78

3. **Tony has a spinner that is equally divided into 6 sections. What is the probability he will land on 1 on his first spin?**
A. $\frac{1}{3}$
B. $\frac{1}{2}$
C. $\frac{2}{3}$
D. $\frac{1}{6}$

4. **Max rolled two identical dice together. What is the probability he will roll a 4 on either one?**
A. $P = (\frac{1}{4})$
B. $P = (\frac{1}{6})$
C. $P = (\frac{1}{12})$
D. $P = (\frac{1}{3})$

5. **Sam and Lee kept team stats for all 8 baseball games. The runs scored were as follows:**

Games:	#1	#2	#3	#4	#5	#6	#7	#8
Scores:	8	4	10	8	5	6	8	9

What was the team's season average?
A. 7.25
B. 8.75
C. 7.5
D. 6.25

6. **Carson's math teacher had everyone select marbles from three boxes, each of which held 16 black and white marbles in different combinations. The drawings below illustrate the assignment and will help you as you complete the table to show the likelihood of Carson's outcomes based on rules of probability.**

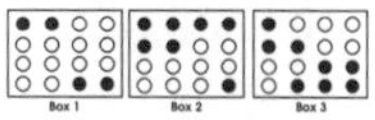
Box 1
Box 2
Box 3

Note: Each selection is tried only once by the students and all marbles are replaced for subsequent selections.

Selection #	Box #	Description	Probability
1	2	only white	$\frac{9}{16}$ or 56%
2	3	white or black	$\frac{16}{16}$ or 100%
3	1	black only	$\frac{4}{16}$ or 25%
4	1 & 3	white only	$\frac{20}{32}$ or 63%

103

page 103

Week 8 • Day 5
Reading for Details

From Boy to President

Do you know any 9-year-olds who have started their own museums? When Theodore Roosevelt was only 9, he and two of his cousins opened the "Roosevelt Museum of Natural History." The museum was in Theodore's bedroom. It had a total of 12 specimens. On display were a few seashells, some dead insects, and some birds' nests. Young Roosevelt took great pride in his small museum.

Born in New York in 1858, Theodore Roosevelt was not always healthy. "I was a sickly, delicate boy," he once wrote. Roosevelt had a health condition called asthma. He often found it hard to breathe. Instead of playing, he observed nature and then read and wrote about it.

Roosevelt's interest in nature sometimes got him into trouble. Once, his mother found several dead mice in the icebox. She demanded that the mice be thrown out. This was indeed "a loss to science," Roosevelt said later.

Because Roosevelt was often sickly as a boy, his body was small and frail. When he was about 12, his father urged him to improve his body. Roosevelt began working out in a gym. He didn't become strong quickly. But he did decide to face life's challenges with a strong spirit. That determination stayed with Roosevelt his whole life. And eventually his body did get strong. As an adult, he was an active, healthy person. He enjoyed adventures, and he loved the outdoors!

In 1900, at the age of 41, Roosevelt was elected Vice President. A year later, President McKinley was shot and killed. Roosevelt became our 26th President. At 42, he was the youngest leader the country had ever had.

Use the information you find in the passage to answer the following questions.

1. **What was the name of Teddy's museum?** Roosevelt Museum of Natural History
2. **How many specimens did the museum contain?** 12
3. **Name the three types of specimens.** seashells, dead insects, birds' nests
4. **What did Teddy Roosevelt's mother once find in her icebox?** dead mice
5. **What health condition did Teddy have as a boy?** asthma
6. **What did Teddy's father encourage him to do?** improve his body
7. **In what year did Theodore Roosevelt become President?** 1901
8. **Who was President when Theodore Roosevelt was Vice President?** McKinley

104

page 104

Week 9

Week 9 • Day 1
Venn Diagram

Data in a Venn Diagram

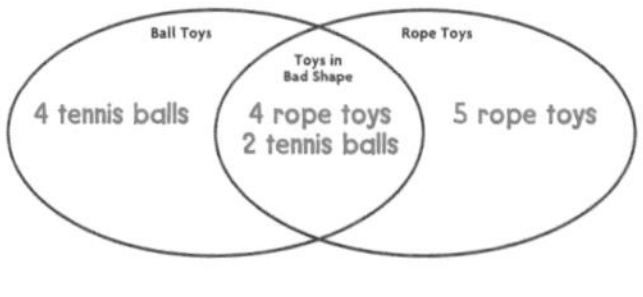
Ball Toys
Rope Toys
Toys in Bad Shape
4 tennis balls
4 rope toys
2 tennis balls
5 rope toys

Maddie's Toy Story

My dog, Maddie, has acquired an affinity for tennis balls and rope toys. When I discovered this, I began to add these to her collection of toys. I spent time each night and on weekends with her playing catch or offering them as chew toys and fetch objects. Eventually, I began to notice her collection of balls and rope toys seemed to be growing rather ragged. So I set out to find and account for the items we had. Here are my findings. From her original treasure trove of 18 tennis balls and 11 rope toys, I found only 15 items. Of the six tennis balls I found, four were still in good shape; the rest were chewed beyond recognition. In the rope toy category, nine remained. Four of those nine rope toys were quite frayed at the ends, while the rest of that number would still do for more fun and games with Maddie.

Organize the story's information in the circle areas of the Venn Diagram based on toy's condition. In the overlap area, there will be a mix of rope toys and tennis balls that are badly chewed. Areas outside the diagram's lines may often be used to show they are similar, but do not fall into one of the categories of the Venn diagram.

1. **Of the 15 toys found, plot data on the diagram to show how each toy will be grouped.**
2. **How many are in the overlap?** 6 **List the types and number.**
4 rope toys and 2 tennis balls
3. **How many balls are not represented on the diagram?** 12 **Explain your answer.**
There were 18, but only 6 were found.
4. **What part of Maddie's 29 toys are not represented on the Venn diagram?** 14

107

page 107

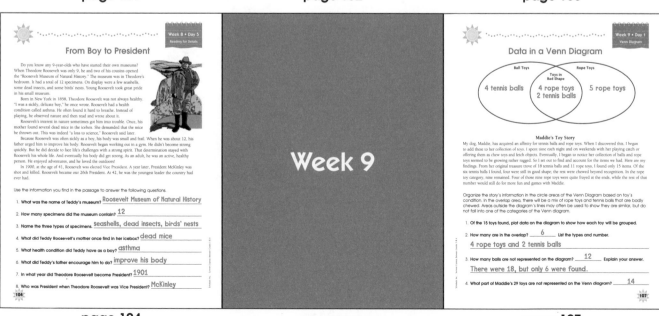

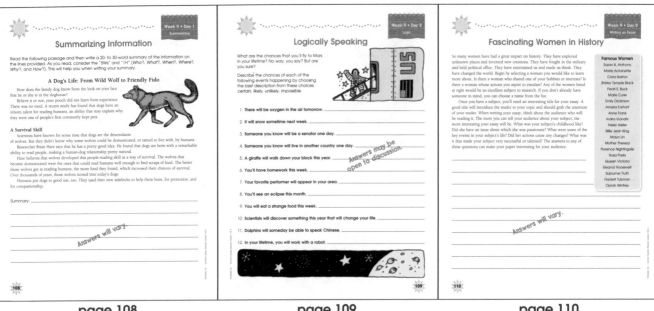

Summarizing Information

Read the following passage and then write a 20- to 30-word summary of the information on the lines provided. As you read, consider the "5Ws" and "1H" (*Who?*, *What?*, *When?*, *Where?*, *Why?*, and *How?*). This will help you when writing your summary.

A Dog's Life: From Wild Wolf to Friendly Fido

How does the family dog know from the look on your face that he or she is in the doghouse?

Believe it or not, your pooch did not learn from experience. There was no need. A recent study has found that dogs have an inborn talent for reading humans, an ability that may explain why they were one of people's first commonly kept pets.

A Survival Skill

Scientists have known for some time that dogs are the descendants of wolves. But they didn't know why some wolves could be domesticated, or tamed to live with, by humans.

Researcher Brian Hare says that he has a pretty good idea. He found that dogs are born with a remarkable ability to read people, making a human-dog relationship pretty natural.

Hare believes that wolves developed this people-reading skill as a way of survival. The wolves that became domesticated were the ones that could read humans well enough to find scraps of food. The better those wolves got at reading humans, the more food they found, which increased their chances of survival. Over thousands of years, those wolves turned into today's dogs.

Humans put dogs to good use, too. They used their new sidekicks to help them hunt, for protection, and for companionship.

Summary: Answers will vary.

page 108

Logically Speaking

What are the chances that you'll fly to Mars in your lifetime? No way, you say? But are you sure?

Describe the chances of each of the following events happening by choosing the best description from these choices: *certain, likely, unlikely, impossible.*

1. **There will be oxygen in the air tomorrow.**
2. **It will snow sometime next week.**
3. **Someone you know will be a senator one day.**
4. **Someone you know will live in another country one day.**
5. **A giraffe will walk down your block this year.**
6. **You'll have homework this week.**
7. **Your favorite performer will appear in your area.**
8. **You'll see an eclipse this month.**
9. **You will eat a strange food this week.**
10. **Scientists will discover something this year that will change your life.**
11. **Dolphins will someday be able to speak Chinese.**
12. **In your lifetime, you will work with a robot.**

Answers may be open to discussion.

page 109

Fascinating Women in History

So many women have had a great impact on history. They have explored unknown places and invented new creations. They have fought in the military and held political office. They have entertained us and made us think. They have changed the world. Begin by selecting a woman you would like to learn more about. Is there a woman who shared one of your hobbies or interests? Is there a woman whose actions you aspire to emulate? Any of the women listed at right would be an excellent subject to research. If you don't already have someone in mind, you can choose a name from the list.

Once you have a subject, you'll need an interesting title for your essay. A good title will introduce the reader to your topic and should grab the attention of your reader. When writing your essay, think about the audience who will be reading it. The more you can tell your audience about your subject, the more interesting your essay will be. What was your subject's childhood like? Did she have an issue about which she was passionate? What were some of the key events in your subject's life? Did her actions cause any changes? What was it that made your subject very successful or talented? The answers to any of these questions can make your paper interesting for your audience.

Famous Women
- Susan B. Anthony
- Marie Antoinette
- Clara Barton
- Shirley Temple Black
- Pearl S. Buck
- Marie Curie
- Emily Dickinson
- Amelia Earhart
- Anne Frank
- Indira Gandhi
- Helen Keller
- Billie Jean King
- Maya Lin
- Mother Theresa
- Florence Nightingale
- Rosa Parks
- Queen Victoria
- Eleanor Roosevelt
- Sojourner Truth
- Harriett Tubman
- Oprah Winfrey

Answers will vary.

page 110

What Does It Mean?

Read the questions carefully. Circle the letter of the answer that is the best choice for the word meaning in that context. If necessary, use a dictionary or thesaurus.

1. **Which of the following remarks does not show reluctance?**
   A. "What's the rush?"
   B. "Let me think about it."
   (C.) "I want to leave now!"
   D. "Well, let's not be too hasty."
2. **In which of the following places would a pedestrian be?**
   A. Sitting on the sofa
   (B.) On the sidewalk
   C. Flying on an airplane
   D. Inside a city bus
3. **Which of the following would you personally not tolerate?**
   A. respect
   B. obedience
   C. an accident
   (D.) deceit
4. **Which of the following might not inspire you to persevere?**
   A. persistence
   (B.) idleness
   C. aspiration
   D. endurance
5. **Which of the following can be breached?**
   A. trick
   B. challenge
   (C.) agreement
   D. vacation
6. **Which one of the following would probably not cause a controversy?**
   A. closing a factory
   (B.) refusing to eat Brussels sprouts
   C. firing the mayor
   D. extending the school year
7. **Which of the following would not be a catastrophe?**
   A. earthquake
   B. hurricane
   C. a plane crash
   (D.) a picnic
8. **Which of the following can be quenched?**
   (A.) thirst
   B. diagram
   C. campfire
   D. ridicule
9. **Which of the following does not exclude even numbers?**
   A. 11, 13, 15, 17
   (B.) 2, 4, 6, 8, 10
   C. 1, 3, 5, 7, 9
   D. 13, 17, 19, 21
10. **Which of the following can be territorial?**
    A. dogwood
    B. treadmill
    C. tennis racket
    (D.) guard dog

page 111

Mapmaker, Mapmaker

On a political map, regions that share borders often have different colors. Mathematicians have proved that no map needs more than four colors. Red, yellow, orange, blue—which four colors would you use to color a map of the world?

Color the maps using only the given number of colors.

1. **Use 3 colors.**

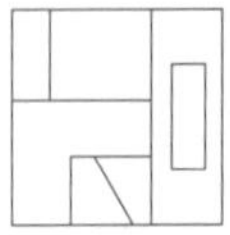

2. **Use 4 colors.**

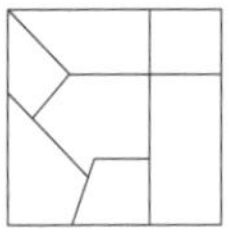

3. **Color this map using 4 colors.**

Answers will vary.

page 112

Find Mistakes—and Fix Them!

Carefully read the following sentences. Add punctuation—commas, semicolons, colons, periods, exclamation points, underlining, and quotation marks—where needed.

1. **Laurie screamed, "Watch out!"**
2. **"One" is the name of my favorite song from the musical A Chorus Line.**
3. **Leslie is the most talented pianist, however she needs more practice.**
4. **Dr. Mauldin announced, "I plan to treat her infections with antibiotics."**
5. **On December 16, 1773, colonists in Boston, Massachusetts, objected to British taxes.**
6. **"Jessica, what can you tell the class about the Boston Tea Party?" asked Mr Starks.**
7. **Did the American Revolution begin on April 19, 1775 ?**
8. **"When do we begin our cruise to the Greek Isles, Turkey, and Spain?" asked Marcus.**
9. **Jennifer lives at 1517 Oak Grove Park, Atlanta, Georgia, 30345.**
10. **The Scott family traveled to the following islands: Grenada, Trinidad, and Martinique.**
11. **"No, Theresa," Peter answered, "the call was not for you."**
12. **Alex, Kevin, Jerry, and Kenny stayed in the basement during the storm.**
13. **The Caspian Sea, the largest lake in the world, has an area of 143,550 square miles.**
14. **Wow! Mrs Porter actually offered Mark a job.**
15. **Douglas asked, "Which route do we take to the Botanical Gardens?"**

page 113

Area Irregulars

Estimate the area enclosed by each irregular shape's outline. To get a reasonable estimate: **1**) Count all the squares that lie completely within the outline. **2**) Count all the squares through which the outline passes; these lie only partially within the outline. Divide this number by 2. **3**) Add the sum from steps 1 and 2.

Answers may vary slightly. Possible answers given.

1.

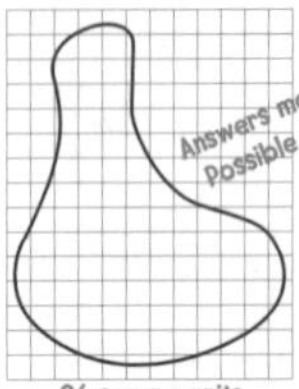

86 square units

3.

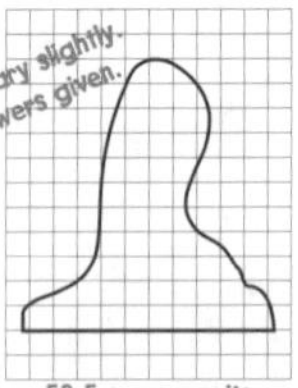

53.5 square units

2.

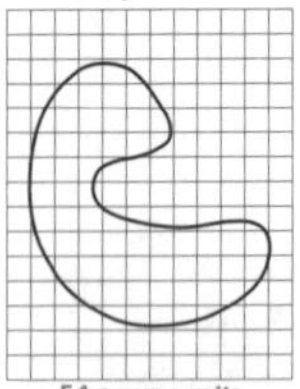

54 square units

4.

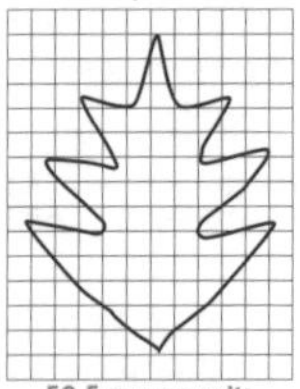

58.5 square units

page 114

The Making of a Major Techie

William Henry Gates, III, was born October 28, 1955, in Seattle, Washington. He grew up in an upper-middle-class family with his older sister, Kristianne, and younger sister, Libby. Their father, William H. Gates, Jr., was a lawyer, and their mother, Mary Maxwell Gates, worked briefly as a teacher. She later gave up teaching to raise her children and work on civic affairs through various charities, including the United Way. She would often take Bill along on her volunteer work in schools and community organizations. Their relationship was a close one and only grew as a result of these shared times of volunteering and meeting people from varied backgrounds.

As a child, Bill showed a variety of interests. He relished playing board games, such as "Risk" and "Monopoly" and was often found reading reference books. His competitive side also came through during athletic games that he organized on summer vacations at the family's summer home on Puget Sound. At age 11 or 12, Bill's behavior in school began to worry his parents. He was doing well, but seemed bored and a bit withdrawn, so his parents enrolled him in Lakeside School at age 13. At Lakeside, Bill began to show enthusiasm for computers and computer programming. He did well in all of his subjects and excelled in math, science, drama, and English.

While at Lakeside School, a Seattle computer company offered to provide computer time for the students. A parents' association used proceeds from the school's rummage sale to purchase a Teletype terminal for students to use. Bill Gates became entranced with what a computer could do and spent much of his free time working at the terminal. He wrote a tic-tac-toe program in BASIC computer language that allowed users to play against the computer.

It was at Lakeside School where Bill met Paul Allen; the two became fast friends, bonding on their common enthusiasm over computers, even though their personalities were very different. Allen was more reserved and shy. Bill was feisty and at times combative. They both spent a great deal of their free time together working on programs. Occasionally, they would clash over who was right about a computer-related question or who should run the computer lab. On one occasion, Gates and Allen had their school computer privileges revoked for taking advantage of software glitches to get more free computer time from the company providing the computers. They were allowed back in the computer lab when they offered to debug the program. Bill later developed a payroll program for that same computer company.

Clearly Bill Gates was destined to develop a software company that spans the globe and attracts high respect from virtually all quarters.

page 115

Use the information you find in the passage to answer the following questions.

1. **What were the names of Bill Gates' sisters?**
   A. Lydia and Kristianne
   (B.) Libby and Kristianne
   C. Mary and Libby
   D. Sarah and Mary
2. **What board game(s) did Bill enjoy playing when he was younger?**
   (A.) Risk and Monopoly
   B. Chutes and Ladders
   C. Monopoly and Chess
   D. Dominoes and Risk
3. **How was Lakeside School important for Bill Gates?**
   A. His mother was on the board of the school.
   B. He and his wife Melinda formed a foundation to help the school.
   (C.) His parents enrolled him at Lakeside because it would be more challenging.
   D. His sisters attended the school and he could be with them.
4. **How would Bill's early relationship with Paul Allen be best described?**
   A. friendly, helpful, and silly
   (B.) cooperative, explosive, and professional
   C. estranged, awkward, and unhelpful
   D. casual, social, and distant
5. **Why was the computer lab at Lakeside important to Bill and Paul?**
   A. The computer lab gave them something to do other than play football.
   B. They had their parents buy the lab for the school.
   C. Bill and Paul broke all of the computers.
   (D.) They began writing computer programs.
6. **What was the name of a computer language Bill used?**
   A. Puget Sound
   B. English
   (C.) BASIC
   D. Teletype
7. **While he was at Lakeside, how did Bill help another company?**
   (A.) Bill created payroll and scheduling programs.
   B. Bill stopped hacking into the computer systems of the school and other businesses.
   C. He created games that the other students could play in their free time.
   D. He donated money to the school.

page 116

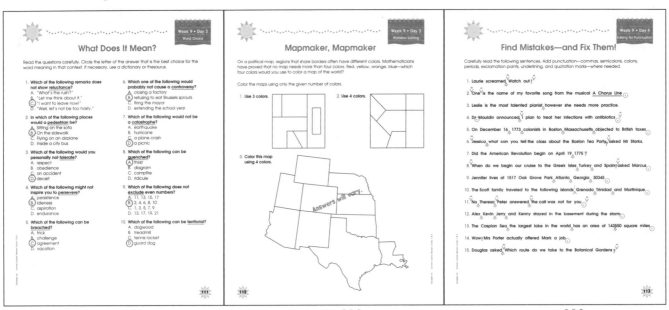

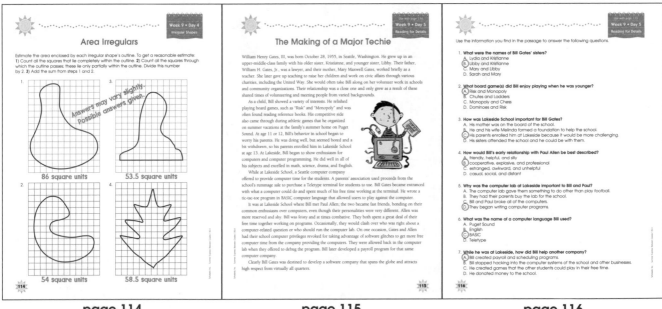

Week 10

---

page 119

Dining at a Mexican Restaurant

Mayra's family is dining at a Mexican restaurant. Use the menu to answer the questions.

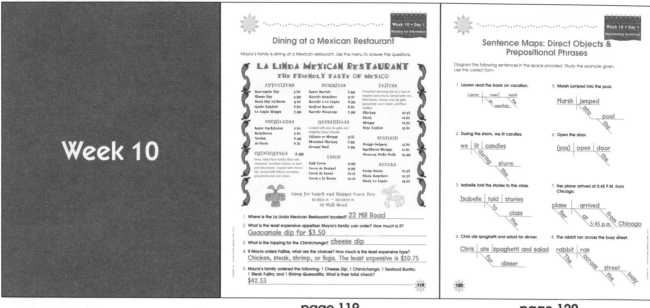

LA LINDA MEXICAN RESTAURANT
THE FRIENDLY TASTE OF MEXICO

Open for Lunch and Dinner Every Day
11:00 a.m. – 10:00 p.m.
22 Mill Road

1. Where is the La Linda Mexican Restaurant located? **22 Mill Road**
2. What is the least expensive appetizer Mayra's family can order? How much is it?
   Guacamole dip for $3.50
3. What is the topping for the Chimichanga? **cheese dip**
4. If Mayra orders Fajitas, what are the choices? How much is the least expensive type?
   Chicken, steak, shrimp, or Baja. The least expensive is $10.75
5. Mayra's family ordered the following: 1 Cheese Dip; 1 Chimichanga; 1 Seafood Burrito; 1 Steak Fajita; and 1 Shrimp Quesadilla. What is their total check?
   $42.53

---

page 120

Sentence Maps: Direct Objects & Prepositional Phrases

Diagram the following sentences in the space provided. Study the example given. Use the correct form.

1. Lauren read the book on vacation.
2. During the storm, we lit candles.
3. Isabelle told the stories to the class.
4. Chris ate spaghetti and salad for dinner.
5. Marsh jumped into the pool.
6. Open the door.
7. Her plane arrived at 5:45 P.M. from Chicago.
8. The rabbit ran across the busy street.

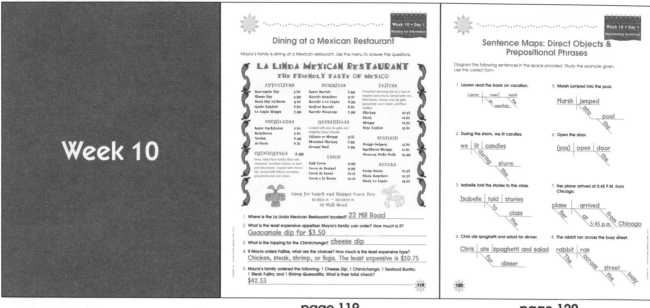

---

page 121

Word Problems—No Problem!

Solve the following word problems. If necessary, use a separate sheet of paper.

1. There were 4 factories that had to fill an order for 412 bicycles. How many bicycles does each factory need to make?
   103
2. Gary purchased a used car. He paid $55 a month for 64 months. How much did he pay in all for the car?
   $3,520.00
3. Kenny has been collecting comic books since the age of 6. He collects about 40 books per year. If Kenny is now 12 years old, about how many comic books does he have?
   240
4. Jane and Sam like to build kites. They're making a diamond kite that will be 20 inches long on each side. What will the kite's perimeter be?
   80 inches
5. Eliot is building a doghouse for his new puppy, Rocket. The doghouse will be 3½ feet tall. How many inches high will it be?
   42 inches
6. The sum of these two numbers is 16. The product of these two numbers is 48. What are the two numbers?
   12 and 4
7. Mr. Porter is installing a round swimming pool. The company says the pool will have a radius of 18 feet. What is the diameter?
   36 feet
8. Corey purchased a trail bike that cost $179.95. He was given a 20% discount. How much money did he save?
   $35.99
9. A major league baseball diamond is a square 90 feet long on each side. What is the perimeter? What is the area?
   P = 360 feet
   A = 8,100 square feet
10. For charity, the track team jumped rope continuously for 10 hours. Taking turns, each member jumped at a pace of 55 times per minute. How many times did they jump rope during 10 hours?
    33,000 times

---

page 122

Figuratively Speaking!

Figurative language is language that means more than what it actually says on the surface. Figurative language can be used to add details to sentences, to add vividness and surprise, to clarify a point, or even to enhance your writing. The four kinds of figurative language are **metaphors, similes, hyperbole,** and **personification.** The two most common figures of speech are similes and metaphors.

- A simile makes a comparison between two unlike things, using like or as.
  Example: She was quiet as a mouse.
- A metaphor makes a comparison between two unlike things, without using like or as.
  Example: The road was a ribbon of moonlight.
- A personification gives human characteristics and qualities to nonhuman things, like animals.
  Example: The moon peeked through the clouds and smiled down on us.
- A hyperbole is an exaggerated statement used to heighten the effect.
  Example: The ice-cream sundae had toppings that were a mile high.

Select the best answer for the following questions.

1. Which of the following is not a figure of speech?
   A. metaphor
   B. simile
   C. alliteration
   D. hyperbole
2. "The old mansion frowned down at us from the top of the hill" is an example of a
   A. metaphor.
   B. personification.
   C. simile.
   D. hyperbole.
3. "She was out like a light" is an example of a
   A. simile.
   B. metaphor.
   C. metaphor.
   D. personification.
4. Figurative language adds which of the following things to your writing?
   A. vividness
   B. surprise
   C. obstacle
   D. A and B
5. "The sea licked the grass at the edge of the shore." This sentence is an example of a
   A. metaphor.
   B. personification.
   C. simile.
   D. hyperbole.
6. Jonathan's feet were houseboats! This sentence is an example of a
   A. metaphor.
   B. personification.
   C. hyperbole.
   D. simile.

---

page 123

Using Pictographs

The following pictographs contain data from the Eagle Woods Middle School's Happy-Gram sales for 2009 and 2010. Use the information shown to answer the questions.

2009 Happy-Gram Sales Data = 24 Happy-Grams

Homeroom	Students Participating	Happy-Grams Sold
Mr. Casey	30	
Mr. Davis	28	
Mrs. Ng	29	
Mrs. Gold	30	
Mrs. Harper	27	
Mrs. Evors	29	

2010 Happy-Gram Sales Data = 24 Happy-Grams

Homeroom	Students Participating	Happy-Grams Sold
Mr. Casey	20	
Mr. Davis	30	
Mrs. Ng	30	
Mrs. Gold	28	
Mrs. Harper	29	
Mrs. Evors	25	

1. The sales in 2009 for Mrs. Evors' homeroom exceeded which class or classes that year?
   A. Mrs. Harper's and Mr. Davis's
   B. Mrs. Ng's, Mrs. Harper's, and Mr. Casey's
   C. Mrs. Gold's and Mrs. Harper's
   D. only Mrs. Gold's
2. All of Mr. Casey's participants sold the same amount in 2009. How many did each participant sell?
   A. 6
   B. 4
   C. 60
   D. 120
3. What is the total sales amount for Mr. Davis' class in 2009 & 2010?
   A. 72
   B. 168
   C. 250
   D. 192
4. Which class sold a total of 240 in both years combined?
   A. Mr. Casey's
   B. Mrs. Harper's
   C. Mr. Davis's
   D. Mrs. Evors'

---

page 124

Inform Your Reader About . . .

Expository writing is a type of writing, the purpose of which is to inform, explain, describe, or define the author's subject to the reader. Expository text is meant to deposit information. Examples of this type of writing are cooking instructions, driving directions, and instructions on performing a task. Key words such as first, after, next, then, and last usually signal sequential writing. The creator of an expository text cannot assume that the reader or listener has prior knowledge or prior understanding of the topic being discussed. One important point to keep in mind is to try to use words that clearly show what you are talking about rather than blatantly telling the reader what is being discussed.

Write an expository paragraph on one of the following topics. Be sure to state your problem and list one or more solutions for the problem. **Remember:** Your task is to inform, explain, describe, or define.

1. Is your school community doing its part to help take care of the environment? Write a paragraph describing how "green" your school really is.
2. Are there problems with our modern day Olympics? Describe things that don't work well and how they might be improved.
3. Can you brainstorm a list of issues that you would like our president to address? What course of action should he take?
4. You have learned this year what it takes to be a fifth grader, what teachers expect of you, and how to succeed as a student. Write a letter that gives fifth grade students specific advice on what they really need to know before they enter sixth grade.

Answers will vary.

---

page 125

What's Your Angle?

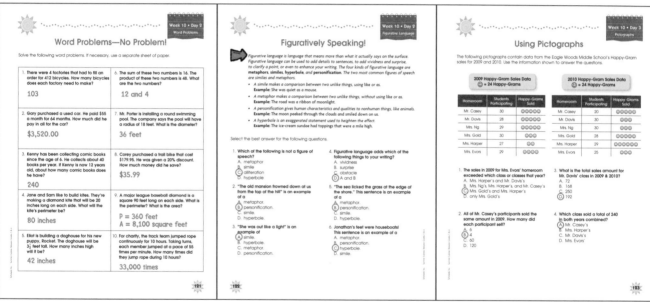

Study the angles above and answer the questions below using what you know about angles. Some questions require the use of a protractor.

1. Which angle is a right angle? **F**
2. What is the measure of a right angle? **90°**
3. List the obtuse angles: **B E**
4. List the acute angles: **A C D G**
5. What is the measurement of angle D? **15°**
6. What is the measurement of angle B? **155°**
7. How much smaller is angle D than angle A? **60°**
8. What would angle A measure if it were increased by 15°? **90°**
9. What would angle E measure if it were decreased 5°? **115°**
10. Draw a 70° angle.

---

page 126

Word Search

Find each of the words in the Word Bank in the puzzle.

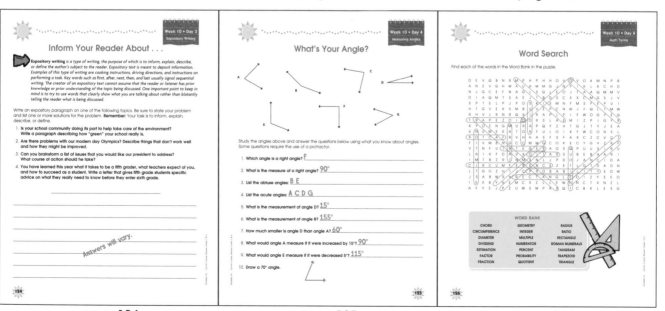

WORD BANK

CHORD	GEOMETRY	RADIUS
CIRCUMFERENCE	INTEGER	RATIO
DIAMETER	MULTIPLE	RECTANGLE
DIVIDEND	NUMERATOR	ROMAN NUMERALS
ESTIMATION	PERCENT	TANGRAM
FACTOR	PROBABILITY	TRAPEZOID
FRACTION	QUOTIENT	TRIANGLE

Triangles

The formula for finding the area of a triangle is $A = \frac{1}{2} \times b \times h$

Example: $A = \frac{1}{2} \times (12 \times 8)$

$A = \frac{1}{2} \times 96$

$A = 48$ sq cm

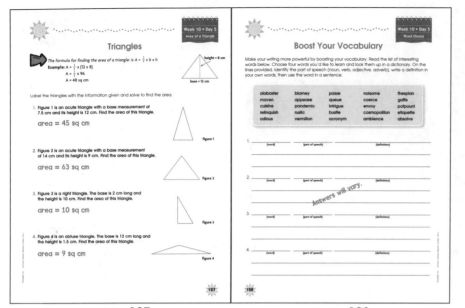

height = 8 cm

base = 12 cm

Label the triangles with the information given and solve to find the area.

1. Figure 1 is an acute triangle with a base measurement of 7.5 cm and its height is 12 cm. Find the area of this triangle.

area = 45 sq cm

figure 1

2. Figure 2 is an acute triangle with a base measurement of 14 cm and its height is 9 cm. Find the area of this triangle.

area = 63 sq cm

figure 2

3. Figure 3 is a right triangle. The base is 2 cm long and the height is 10 cm. Find the area of this triangle.

area = 10 sq cm

figure 3

4. Figure 4 is an obtuse triangle. The base is 12 cm long and the height is 1.5 cm. Find the area of this triangle.

area = 9 sq cm

figure 4

Boost Your Vocabulary

Make your writing more powerful by boosting your vocabulary. Read the list of interesting words below. Choose four words you'd like to learn and look them up in a dictionary. On the lines provided, identify the part of speech (noun, verb, adjective, adverb), write a definition in your own words, then use the word in a sentence.

alabaster	blarney	passe	noisome	thespian
maven	appease	queue	coerce	gaffe
cuisine	pandemic	intrigue	envoy	potpourri
relinquish	rustic	bustle	cosmopolitan	etiquette
odious	vermilion	acronym	ambience	absolve

1. _____ (word) _____ (part of speech) _____ (definition)

2. _____ (word) _____ (part of speech) _____ (definition)

Answers will vary.

3. _____ (word) _____ (part of speech) _____ (definition)

4. _____ (word) _____ (part of speech) _____ (definition)

THIS CERTIFIES THAT

IS NOW READY

FOR GRADE _____

CONGRATULATIONS!

I'm proud of you!